MYSTERIES, LEGENDS, AND UNEXPLAINED PHENOMENA

ESP, PSYCHOKINESIS, AND PSYCHICS

MYSTERIES, LEGENDS, AND UNEXPLAINED PHENOMENA

MYSTERIES, LEGENDS, AND UNEXPLAINED PHENOMENA

ESP, PSYCHOKINESIS, AND PSYCHICS

JOANNE P. AUSTIN
Consulting Editor: Rosemary Ellen Guiley

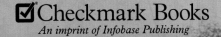

Checkmark Books
An imprint of Infobase Publishing

ESP, PSYCHOKINESIS, AND PSYCHICS

Checkmark Books
An imprint of Infobase Publishing
132 West 31st Street
New York NY 10001

ISBN-13: 978-1-60413-316-5
ISBN-10: 1-6041-3316-3

Library of Congress has cataloged the hardcover edition as follows:
Austin, Joanne.
ESP, psychokinesis, and psychics / Joanne P. Austin ; consulting editor, Rosemary Ellen Guiley.
     p. cm. — (Mysteries, legends, and unexplained phenomena)
  Includes bibliographical references and index.
  ISBN-13: 978-0-7910-9388-7 (alk. paper)
  ISBN-10: 0-7910-9388-3 (alk. paper)
  1. Parapsychology. 2. Extrasensory perception. 3. Psychokinesis. 4. Psychics. I. Guiley, Rosemary. II. Title. III. Series.
  BF1001.A88 2007
  133.8—dc22
                              2007023009

Text design by James Scotto-Lavino
Cover design by Ben Peterson

Printed in the United States of America

Bang EJB 10 9 8 7 6 5 4 3 2 1

This book is printed on acid-free paper.

Contents

Foreword

Did you ever have an experience that turned your whole world upside down? Maybe you saw a ghost or a UFO. Perhaps you had an unusual, vivid dream that seemed real. Maybe you suddenly knew that a certain event was going to happen in the future. Or, perhaps you saw a creature or a being that did not fit the description of anything known in the natural world. At first you might have thought your imagination was playing tricks on you. Then, perhaps, you wondered about what you experienced and went looking for an explanation.

Every day and night people have experiences they can't explain. For many people these events are life changing. Their comfort zone of what they can accept as "real" is put to the test. It takes only one such experience for people to question the reality of the mysterious worlds that might exist beyond the one we live in. Perhaps you haven't encountered the unknown, but you have an intense curiosity about it. Either way, by picking up this book you've started an adventure to explore and learn more, and you've come to the right place! The book you hold has been written by a leading expert in the paranormal—someone who understands unusual experiences and who knows the answers to your questions.

As a seeker of knowledge, you have plenty of company. Mythology, folklore, and records of the past show that human beings have had paranormal experiences throughout history. Even prehistoric cave paintings and gravesites indicate that early humans had concepts of the supernatural and of an afterlife. Humans have always sought to understand paranormal experiences and to put them into a frame of reference that makes sense to us in our daily lives. Some of the greatest minds in history have grappled with questions about the paranormal. For example, Greek philosopher Plato pondered the nature of dreams and how we "travel" during them. Isaac Newton was interested in the esoteric study of alchemy, which has magical elements, and St. Thomas Aquinas explored the nature of angels and spirits. Philosopher William James joined organizations dedicated to psychical research, and even the inventor of the light bulb, Thomas Alva Edison, wanted to build a device that could talk to the dead. More recently physicists such as David Bohm, Stephen Hawking, William Tiller, and Michio Kaku have developed ideas that may help explain how and why paranormal phenomena happen, and neuroscience researchers like Michael Persinger have explored the nature of consciousness.

Exactly what is a paranormal experience or phenomenon? "Para" is derived from a Latin term for "beyond." So "paranormal" means "beyond normal," or things that do not fit what we experience through our five senses alone and which do not follow the laws we observe in nature and in science. Paranormal experiences and phenomena run the gamut from the awesome and marvelous, such as angels and miracles, to the downright terrifying, such as vampires and werewolves.

Paranormal experiences have been consistent throughout the ages, but explanations of them have changed as societies, cultures, and technologies have changed. For example, our ancestors were much closer to the invisible realms. In times when life was simpler, they saw, felt, and experienced other realities on a daily basis. When night fell, the darkness was thick and quiet, and it was easier to see unusual things, such as ghosts. They had no electricity to keep the night lit up. They had no media for constant communication and entertainment. Travel was difficult. They had more time to notice subtle things that were just beyond their ordinary senses. Few doubted their experiences. They accepted the invisible realms as an extension of ordinary life.

Today we have many distractions. We are constantly busy from the time we wake up until we go to bed. The world is full of light and noise 24 hours a day, seven days a week. We have television, the

Internet, computer games, and cell phones to keep us busy, busy, busy. We are ruled by technology and science. Yet, we still have paranormal experiences very similar to those of our ancestors. Because these occurrences do not fit neatly into science and technology, many people think they are illusions, and there are plenty of skeptics always ready to debunk the paranormal and reinforce that idea.

In roughly the past 100 years, though, some scientists have studied the paranormal and attempted to find scientific evidence for it. Psychic phenomena have proven difficult to observe and measure according to scientific standards. However, lack of scientific proof does not mean paranormal experiences do not happen. Courageous scientists are still looking for bridges between science and the supernatural.

My personal experiences are behind my lifelong study of the paranormal. Like many children I had invisible playmates when I was very young, and I saw strange lights in the yard and woods that I instinctively knew were the nature spirits who lived there. Children seem to be very open to paranormal phenomena, but their ability to have these experiences often fades away as they become more involved in the outside world, or, perhaps, as adults tell them not to believe in what they experience, that it's only in their imagination. Even when I was very young, I was puzzled that other people would tell me with great authority that I did not experience what I knew I did.

A major reason for my interest in the paranormal is precognitive dreaming experienced by members of my family. Precognition means "fore knowing," or knowing the future. My mother had a lot of psychic experiences, including dreams of future events. As a teen it seemed amazing to me that dreams could show us the future. I was determined to learn more about this and to have such dreams myself. I found books that explained extrasensory perception, the knowing of information beyond the five senses. I learned about dreams and experimented with them. I taught myself to visit distant places in my dreams and to notice details about them that I could later verify in the physical world. I learned how to send people telepathic messages in dreams and how to receive messages in dreams. Every night became an exciting adventure.

Those interests led me to other areas of the paranormal. Pretty soon I was engrossed in studying all kinds of topics. I learned different techniques for divination, including the Tarot. I learned how to meditate. I took courses to develop my own psychic skills, and I gave psychic readings to others. Everyone has at least some natural psychic ability and can improve it with attention and practice.

Next I turned my attention to the skies, to ufology, and what might be "out there" in space. I studied the lore of angels and fairies. I delved into the dark shadowy realm of demons and monsters. I learned the principles of real magic and spell casting. I undertook investigations of haunted places. I learned how to see auras and do energy healing. I even participated in some formal scientific laboratory experiments for telepathy.

My studies led me to have many kinds of experiences that have enriched my understanding of the paranormal. I cannot say that I can prove anything in scientific terms. It may be some time yet before science and the paranormal stop flirting with each other and really get together. Meanwhile, we can still learn a great deal from our personal experiences. At the very least, our paranormal experiences contribute to our inner wisdom. I encourage others to do the same as I do. Look first for natural explanations of strange phenomena. If natural explanations cannot be found or seem unlikely, consider paranormal explanations. Many paranormal experiences fall into a vague area, where although a natural cause might exist, we simply don't know what could explain them. In that case I tell people to trust their intuition that they had a paranormal experience. Sometimes the explanation makes itself known later on.

I have concluded from my studies and experiences that invisible dimensions are layered upon our world, and that many paranormal experiences occur when there are openings between worlds. The doorways often open at unexpected times. You take a trip, visit a haunted place, or have a strange dream–and suddenly reality shifts. You get a glimpse behind the curtain that separates the ordinary from the extraordinary.

The books in this series will introduce you to these exciting and mysterious subjects. You'll learn many things that will astonish you. You'll be given lots of tips for how to explore the paranormal on your own. Paranormal investigation is a popular field, and you don't have to be a scientist or a full-time researcher to explore it. There are many things you can do in your free time. The knowledge you gain from these books will help prepare you for any unusual and unexpected experiences.

As you go deeper into your study of the paranormal, you may come up with new ideas for explanations. That's one of the appealing aspects of paranormal investigation–there is always room for bold ideas. So, keep an open and curious mind, and think big. Mysterious worlds are waiting for you!

—Rosemary Ellen Guiley

Introduction

"Eeenie, meenie, chili beanie—the spirits are about to speak."
—Bullwinkle J. Moose

In the classic cartoon series *The Bullwinkle Show*, there was a recurring joke that showed the ever-hopeful Bullwinkle gazing into his crystal ball, certain that this time he would make contact with the Other Side. Unfortunately, no matter how many times he tried, Bullwinkle never heard from anyone.[1]

Unlike Bullwinkle, though, there are people that *do* possess a so-called sixth sense and are able to know things that the rest of the population either doesn't pick up on or chooses to ignore. These individuals, known as psychics, display an exceptional ability to gain knowledge from a source beyond the five senses of sight, hearing, smell, touch, and taste.

Historically, anyone who received messages in dreams or trances, heard voices, and maybe foretold the future was either revered as a priest or shaman who had been touched by the divine or else was shunned as a nut case. Crazy or not, however, the seer would often be consulted by the leader (maybe a king) of his tribe or others in hopes of receiving answers to the questions that affected their lives: Will we be victorious in battle? Will the harvest or hunt be bountiful? Will the goatherder's daughter be my wife? And so the priest or shaman would consult his bones or the stars or maybe take a deep drag on his pipe and wait to get a mental picture for what might happen. Realizing the benefit of a little razzle-dazzle, the shaman would captivate the group with dancing, singing, and wise pronouncements. The shaman's life probably depended on the accuracy of his powers, which helps explain why psychic revelations often are vague. Being psychic was risky then, and it still is.

PSYCHICS: WHO ARE THEY, WHAT DO THEY DO, AND HOW DO THEY DO IT?

So who are these people who can find that misplaced $20 bill by "seeing" it in the glove compartment of the car? Or even more amazing, can alter events that have already happened?

Chapter One explains how psychics have been part of the human landscape for thousands of years, claiming to foresee the future and interpret the will of the divine. In the 1930s, pioneer researcher J. B. Rhine defined these unexplained gifts as powers of **extrasensory perception (ESP)** and **psychokinesis (PK)**.

Since the 1940s, however, the idea that **paranormal** (beyond normal) ability depended on a person's perception or action has made scientists uncomfortable. Searching for a more general term, they adopted the word **psi**.[2] Although principally concerned with ESP and PK, psi also refers to other types of unexplained energy such as psychic healing and poltergeist activity and, broadly defined, encompasses any type of paranormal activity such as ghosthunting.[3]

Chapter Two explores some of the ways psychic phenomena appear, including the accounts of two famous poltergeist cases and what happened to the girls at the center of all the uproar. This section also examines research experiments on ESP and PK, including Ganzfield simulations, spoon bending, and psychometry.

Although a good psychic may not need props in order to receive or send messages, Chapter Three summarizes some of the aids available to facilitate a reading, including Tarot cards, astrology, palm reading, automatic writing, crystals, smooth surfaces, and Ouija boards or other planchette devices.

PSYCHIC NATION

Psychics are everywhere: giving sittings at fairs, appearing on television and talk radio, producing their own TV programs, writing books, leading seminars, solving crimes, and offering readings over the telephone.

Chapter Five takes a brief look at modern psychic heavyweights such as James Van Praagh, John Edward, Allison DuBois, and Sylvia Browne, as well as the media machine that supports them. People can't seem to get enough of all things paranormal. Even Disney has taken the sketchy stories that describe their haunted-house attractions and twisted them into films.

And based on the public's fascination with psychic crimefighting, perhaps law enforcement agencies have softened their stand against participation by profilers. Television programs such as *Psychic Detectives* showcase the increased involvement of psychics in criminal investigations, especially in missing-person cases.

PROVING THE EXISTENCE OF PSI

By the mid-nineteenth century, many Americans and Europeans believed wholeheartedly in the existence of paranormal phenomena. Chapter Four provides background on historical psychics such as Nostradamus, whose precognitive revelations continue to baffle modern historians; Emanuel Swedenborg, a remote viewer who saw visions of Heaven; Edgar Cayce, whose astounding healing gifts were never fully understood; Leonora Piper, a gifted psychic who convinced philosopher William James that paranormal communication was possible; and Jeane Dixon, who claimed to have predicted the assassination of President John F. Kennedy.

Outlandish claims of psychic ability gave rise to the formation of societies and organizations devoted to the verification of a psychic's powers. Chapters Six and Seven cover the history of paranormal investigation, from the founding of the Society for Psychical Research in London (1882) to the skepticism of those magicians and scientists who believe demonstrations of phenomena are no more than skillful acts.

BECOMING PSYCHIC

It appears that anyone can develop some level of psi with study and practice. Classes and entire curricula have been developed to teach the interested to become the proficient. Chapter Eight lists some of the signs to look for that indicate a sixth sense and examines a few of the methods used to produce a psychic, as well as the pitfalls to avoid.

TALKING AND LISTENING TO THE ANIMALS

Finally, how do some dogs always know when their owners are on the way home? Some cats, too, have this gift. One of the most highly studied dogs with extraordinary paranormal gifts was a terrier named Jaytee who lived in England. Then there are the pet psychics, claiming they can get the real story straight from the horse's mouth (so to speak). And last but not least, even plants are psychic. Chapter Nine looks at these amazing abilities.

Psychics: Who Are They and What Do They Do?

Close your eyes . . . and try to visualize the 10-year epic war between ancient Greece and Troy as described by the Greek poet Homer in *The Iliad* (or portrayed in the movie *Troy* with Brad Pitt). The whole mess started because Eris, the goddess of discord, didn't get invited to a party. To get back at the popular crowd, she crashed the wedding of King Peleus and Thetis and threw a golden apple designated "for the fairest" into the middle of the banquet hall. Trojan prince Paris chose Aphrodite, goddess of beauty and love, over the other two contestants, Hera and Athena, because Aphrodite offered him the most beautiful woman in the world, Helen, as his prize. Unfortunately, the lovely Helen was already the wife of King Menelaus of Sparta. Menelaus and the other Greek kings sailed to Troy to retrieve her from Paris[4] (hence the phrase "the face that launched a thousand ships"). The rest is history.

So what does the Judgment of Paris have to do with psychics? Well, Cassandra, Paris's sister, was a psychic and a prophetess. She was also very beautiful. The god Apollo was completely taken with Cassandra and gave her the gift of second sight as proof of his devotion. Cassandra, however, knew Apollo to be a fickle lover, and she declined his advances. He, in turn, twisted his gift so that even though Cassandra would have foreknowledge of every tragedy to befall Troy, no one would believe her.

As the Greeks sacked Troy, Cassandra tried to find sanctuary at the statue of Athena, but the goddess, still angry that she didn't win the contest, allowed the soldiers to drag Cassandra out of the temple and offer her as booty to King Agamemnon, Menelaus' brother. When Agamemnon returned home and casually instructed his wife, Clytemnestra, to see to his slave's needs, Clytemnestra murdered them both.[5]

Nowadays, a "Cassandra" is one who predicts failure and ruin and usually receives ridicule in return. Having psychic ability is no guarantee of popularity.

Cassandra was hardly the first seer in history, however—just one of the most reviled. Those who professed to see the future or who had a connection to the world beyond the one people could interpret with their five senses have been a part of culture since the very earliest days of mankind. The reasons those people existed remain central to the human condition today and reinforce the bond between psychic knowledge and religious faith. To foresee what may lie ahead softens the pain, just a little, of what will definitely be in the future: death.

Evidence of mankind on earth—specifically in Africa—goes back at least 2.5 million years. It's not known if those early tribespeople designated a priest or shaman who possessed the power of prophecy. It's likely they did, however, for the native religions encountered by the European explorers, slave traders, and missionaries were steeped in magic and belief in the paranormal. The Chinese, who settled along the Yellow River about 10,000 BCE (Before the Common Era), used deer and oxen bones or tortoise shells—"dragon bones"—to prophesy through contact with dead ancestors.[6] Their divination sticks, the *I Ching*, were in use by approximately 1000 BCE. Ancient Egyptians first started astrological charting around 3100 BCE, while the earliest written records of prophecy in Mesopotamia are about 20 centuries old.[7]

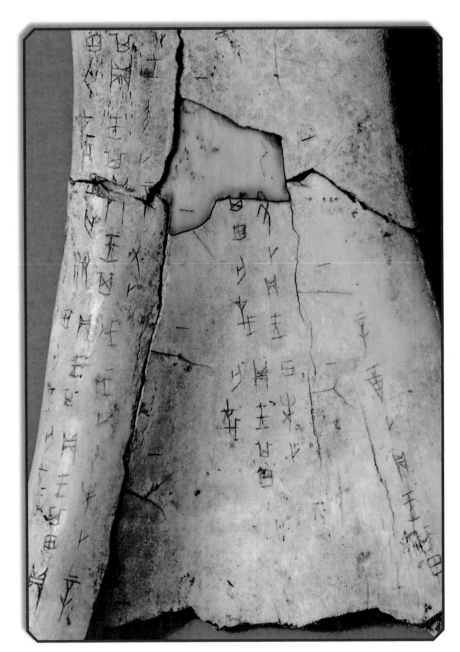

Figure 1.1 *Some oracles used bones in their search for answers, as in the Chinese oracle bone seen here inscribed with questions.* (Lowell Georgia/CORBIS)

By the time Cassandra prophesied the sack of Troy, about 1193 BCE, Delphi had already been a religious location. It became a temple to Apollo in the eighth century BCE. The priestess Pythia answered questions, gave instructions or orders, or predicted the future while in trance—probably as the result of ethylene fumes seeping up from the ground, according to archeological research.[8]

For the Israelites, the designation of "prophet" carried considerable weight during the early Old Testament period. Prophets such as Moses, Samuel, Hosea, Joshua, Jeremiah, Deborah, and Miriam were bridges between the human and the divine. Records show the prophetic tradition was established by the eleventh century BCE and flourished from about 680–627 BCE. By the time of the latter Old Testament, however, Amos, Isaiah, and Micah were not called prophets but visionaries, and after the Exile in Babylonia (587–556 BCE), controversy over whether these visionaries were divinely inspired or demonically possessed led to the decline of the prophecy period.[9]

Prophesying was a gift of the spirit in the early Christian church, useful for interpreting the life of Christ and speculating on the end of days. Saint Paul included such ability in his first letter to the Corinthians (I Corinthians 12:10). Saint Augustine and Saint Isidore of Seville both studied telepathy.[10] Unfortunately, so many got into the prophesying business, many of them frauds, that Church fathers eventually turned against the gift, characterizing prophesying as the Devil's work and effectively suppressing its practitioners.[11] In the eighteenth century, Pope Benedict XIV investigated paranormal activity and concluded that such experiences were neither demonic nor divine.[12]

WHAT ARE PSYCHIC PHENOMENA?

So the history is interesting, but what does it have to do with psychic phenomena? Everything. Ancient records point to a belief in and reliance upon those who exhibited *psi*: the power to "know" by some way other than the five senses of touch, sight, hearing, taste, and smell.

In the first half of the twentieth century, researchers described psychics as persons exhibiting two types of paranormal activity: ESP and PK. By the mid-1940s, psychic researchers Richard H. Thouless, former president of the Society for Psychical Research, and biochemist B. P. Weisner became uncomfortable with the specific nature of "perception" and adopted the word psi as a more general term not tied to cause and effect.[13] Although Thouless and Weisner did not intend for psi to cover all unexplained phenomena, the word has come to represent anything paranormal. Nevertheless, ESP and PK remain the two most important features of psi.

Psi is the 23rd letter of the Greek alphabet (it looks like this: Ψ). It is the first letter of words that have Greek roots like *psychology* and *psychic* and *psycho*—terms that pertain to human behavior. The translation actually means "breath" or "soul."[14]

Generally speaking, there are three ways to become psychic: a head injury or some other severe emotional or physical trauma, a genetic inheritance from an ancestor in one's family, or by study and practice. The manifestation of paranormal sensitivity—hearing voices and seeing visions—in someone who has not experienced it before can be quite frightening and could be mistaken for insanity. While interviewing author and parapsychologist Dean Radin, Jordan S. Gruber admits that even though he believes in psi, he'd probably have a heart attack from shock if he discovered he could **levitate** an object.[15] Mental illness sometimes accompanies psi ability. Too often, psychics are abused by skeptics or ignorant people and retreat into dissociative behaviors (what used to be called split personalities).[16]

The most talented psychics inherit psi from a relative, although that family member has no control over who receives the gift or whether it passes to the next generation or skips to the one after. People without benefit of psychic ancestors or who haven't suffered a concussion can develop some level of psychic ability through reading the literature and practicing on their friends and family, but it is unlikely that they will be as proficient as those in the first two categories. Radin estimates that only half of one percent of all psychics are high-functioning, meaning those who are very sensitive, competent, and tuned in to paranormal energy. [17]

PRACTICAL PSI

If exhibiting psi is an art, not a science (and an arbitrary one at that), is it possible for the psychic to make a mistake or fail to see an impending tragedy—like the terrorist attack on the World Trade Center in New York on September 11, 2001—and still be considered credible? If all the prominent psychics put their heads together, speculates Benjamin Radford, managing editor of the magazine *Skeptical Inquirer*, why can't they locate Osama bin Laden, mastermind of the attack?[18] Do psychics have the paranormal equivalent of a baseball batting average: the number of times a psychic nails a reading or, on the flip side, strikes out?

Skeptics point to the many times a psychic gets a reading wrong as proof that psi is just a parlor trick. The psychic —defensive about the times he or she hit a homer, so to speak—may withdraw and dismiss any question about psi as a personal affront.

Parapsychologist Jeffrey Mishlove argues that proving psi is pointless. How it's used, called **applied psi**, is what counts. After all, the ancient shamans and soothsayers used their psychic abilities to heal, cast spells, and foretell events. Successful executives often rely on intuition in their business dealings. Researchers have studied applied psi in various fields, particularly finance and the stock and commodities markets, but although intuition can be dead-on some of the time, it is also unreliable.[19]

Psychic ability is probably like many other creative talents—being really good at math, playing an instrument, writing a great book, or painting a masterpiece. Some days are inspired, yet on other days the creative juices just don't flow.

Psychic Abilities, or
How Do They Do That?

Imagine that . . . you are 11 years old, the youngest child in your family, and the only one still at home. Your mom and dad decide to move from your farm in Ireland to Sauchie, Scotland, to live near your brother Thomas and his family. Your name is Virginia Campbell, and you are quite shy. You have a dog, Toby, and one friend, Anna.

The year is 1960, and economic conditions in Ireland and Scotland are tough. You and your mom go on to Scotland, while your dad stays behind to settle the sale of the farm. Your mom leaves you at your brother's house to take a job in a nearby town. You like your brother and his family—he has a nine-year-old daughter, Margaret, and a six-year-old son, Derek—but the house is small, and you have to share a double bed, not just a bedroom, with Margaret. You have difficulty fitting in at your new school, you miss your friend Anna, and you don't know when your parents will be settled.

On top of everything else, your body starts changing, and you're too shy to ask anyone what's happening. It's embarrassing to sleep with Margaret; she's still a little girl and you are her aunt, for heaven's sake. Suddenly, one night in late November, "thunking" noises start coming from your bedroom, then knocking sounds. You and Margaret are frightened, especially when the loud knocks seem to warn Margaret to stay out of the bed. Even scarier, big, heavy pieces of furniture start moving across the floor by themselves. School desks levitate. Neighbors, the family doctor, and a pastor come to see the strange phenomena and examine you to see if you're somehow behind all these strange events. But no one can explain them.[20]

What's going on? Commonly referred to as **poltergeist** (German for "noisy ghost") phenomena, the noises and moving furniture are manifestations of psychokinesis (PK).[21] Poltergeist phenomena have been known to include pictures swinging wildly on their wires, mirrors shattering, appliances inexplicably turning on by themselves, faucets refusing to stop running, and even telephones flying about the room, giving "mobile phone" a whole new definition! Such amazing phenomena, attributed to ghosts or witches in the old days, now seem to be connected to the intense energy surrounding adolescents and young adults, especially if they are unhappy at home or feel repressed in some way.

In Virginia's case (a true story called the Sauchie Poltergeist), she was dealing with moving to a strange town and school, having to share space with her nine-year-old niece, not knowing when she and her parents would be living together again, and entering puberty. It was more than Virginia could handle, and her frustrations were so overpowering that they took on a life of their own, expressing themselves through extraordinary displays. While Virginia was not directly responsible for the phenomena, she was the human agent at the center of the uproar.

THE TWO SIDES OF PSI

In his book *How to Test and Develop Your ESP*, author Paul Huson draws an analogy between the two types of psi—ESP and PK—and radio. A person with ESP is like a radio receiver, accepting the "signals" out there, while someone causing PK is a radio transmitter, sending out psychic energy and shaking things up.[22] One can be a receiver or a transmitter or both.

The Tragedy of Tina Resch

Tina Resch was at the center of one of the most widely documented episodes of poltergeist activity in the United States. Her sad story stands as a textbook case supporting the existence of *recurrent spontaneous psychokinesis* (RSPK).[23]

Tina was born in October 1969, and her mother abandoned her about a year later. Her foster parents, John and Joan Resch of Columbus, Ohio, adopted Tina; they had older children of their own, an adopted son, Jack, and other foster kids.

School was tough for Tina. She was clumsy and often got into trouble. Instead of helping Tina, her teachers made an example of her and complained about her behavior. The other kids picked on her. Things were no better at home. The Resches were strict and believed in corporal punishment. After her parents decided to homeschool Tina, she hardly ever left the house and had no friends. She also likely suffered from Tourette's Syndrome, a condition that causes jerky movements, nervous tics, and uncontrollable outbursts of loud and sometimes obscene language. She fought with her parents often, leading to more punishment.

On March 1, 1984, after yet another fight, Tina (now 14) threatened John with a knife if he ever hit her again. The next morning, strange things started to happen. Pictures swung on their wires, candleholders rocked back and forth, glassware shattered, unplugged lights and appliances turned on, and furniture moved unaided. The telephone rang constantly and flew around the room.

The Resches called their friend Mike Harden at the *Columbus Dispatch*, who put them in contact with Dr. William G. Roll, founder of the Psychical Research Foundation (PRF). Roll agreed to come to Columbus and observe the phenomena, where he concluded that Tina's

(continues)

(continued)

unbearable home situation and her Tourette's had combined to create the energy that led to the RSPK.[24]

By the time Tina was 16, the RSPK episodes had ceased, but her story didn't end there. The Resches decided to give up parental rights and commit Tina to a juvenile detention facility. To prevent her from becoming a ward of the state, Tina's boyfriend married her, but he beat Tina and she divorced him. In September 1988, Tina gave birth to a little girl, Amber. Tina remarried, but her new husband was also a batterer.

Roll was no longer studying Tina, but they had kept in touch, and he invited her to move to Carrolton, Georgia, where he had relocated the PRF. Tina thought her life was turning around, until Amber died of abuse in April 1992. Although Roll tried to act on her behalf, Tina was tried and convicted of Amber's murder. She is currently serving a life sentence plus 20 years with no parole.

Dr. Roll documented this sad tale in *Unleashed: Of Poltergeists and Murder, the Curious Story of Tina Resch.*

Researcher J. B. Rhine used the term "extrasensory perception" in the 1930s to explain the results of his forced-choice card tests (see Chapter Six), attributing his subjects' ability to successfully identify the symbols on the cards as a natural, but beyond normal (paranormal), use of the five senses. Scientists now divide ESP into three ways of "knowing": **telepathy**, **clairvoyance**, and **precognition**.

Telepathy is knowing another's thoughts, reading minds, and projecting thought or understanding. Such empathy could be attributed to coincidence or familiarity but not always. What would life be like if a person could read everyone's mind? There would be no privacy, no polite discretion. So many voices crowding for attention would eventually just become head-exploding noise.

Clairvoyance (from the French for "clear-seeing"), the second form of ESP, is commonly called "second sight" or the sixth sense. Some psychics describe this gift as seeing with an "inner" or "third eye." Visions can be spontaneous and immediate or the result of dreams or trances. Huson, returning to his electronics analogy, says clairvoyance is more like radar than radio. The psychic perceives a cluster of impressions associated with things or people previously associated with the subject, not anything that the subject is directly thinking or "transmitting."[25]

Although associated with visions, clairvoyance also encompasses other forms of psychic perception. **Clairsentience**, or "clear-knowing," refers to receiving psychic impressions with no accompanying natural sensory impressions. **Clairaudience** ("clear-hearing") describes psychic audio, not video. It's like a little voice in your head but different from one's conscience. Closely associated with trance states, clairaudience can occur while dreaming or under hypnosis. The phenomenon may manifest in times of crisis, alerting the hearer to a loved one's tragic or even fatal circumstances.[26]

Another form of clairvoyance is **psychometry**, or the ability to discern information about persons, places, or events just by holding an object associated with them.[27] Most psychic criminologists claim proficiency in psychometry, which is especially useful in missing-person cases. Psychometry also figures prominently in psychic archaeology, or sensing information about the locations of ruins by holding a relic or even a photo of a site.[28]

All of these extraordinary abilities are fascinating, but many people would really like to know whether there is any connection between psi and luck. Imagine how cool it would be to know in advance the winning lottery numbers or what stocks were going to jump.

A study in England starting about the year 2000 conducted by computer programmer Mick O'Neill, a member of the Society for

Psychical Research, looked at whether psi could be used to pick winning numbers in the British National Lottery, which pays out about £100 million, approximately $200 million each year. Volunteers visualized as many lottery numbers as possible and submitted them to O'Neill, who bought tickets on their behalf. There was no cost to participate or commitment to play, and if a ticket won, the volunteer shared in the winnings.

The goal was to have the group so attuned that it would beat the odds and share in a big jackpot more than once. One player had four winners in 13 months, overcoming odds of three million to one, and several have picked enough winning numbers to get back more than a dollar for every dollar bet.

Interestingly, the stars seem to smile on numbers selected at about 13:30 local sidereal time (LST). Sidereal time is not the same as regular time but instead refers to the movements of the constellations, particularly Libra. When Libra is overhead—any place on Earth—the LST is about 13:30. Physicist James Spottiswoode noticed this anomaly in 1997 but could not explain it.[29] Apparently, it's a favorable time to buy a lottery ticket.

PRECOGNITION AND DREAMS

The final ESP category is *precognition*, which means "foreknowledge" or "knowing before." How can precognition be measured? Huson outlines one experiment conducted in 1969 by parapsychologists Stanley Krippner, Montague Ullmann, and Charles Honorton. In the laboratory, English psychic Malcolm Bessent carefully recorded the vivid dreams he experienced over eight consecutive nights. Then another experimenter, totally unaware of Bessent's dreams, was given props, costumes, art prints, and music to act out eight "scenes." When Bessent's dreams were compared to the scenes, Bessent had foreseen five out of eight![30]

Dreams may be the most popular form of precognition and are not limited to those individuals who claim psychic powers. In the television show *Medium*, the character of psychic Allison DuBois receives most of her information through long, detailed dreams. The real-life DuBois, however, says she usually receives her impressions while awake.[31]

In most spiritual traditions worldwide, people believe that dreams serve as a means for the dead to communicate with the living, offering conflict intervention, delivering advice, and providing proof of survival. The dead also appear to their loved ones to request a more fitting burial, to reveal the hidden location of a secret will, or in some cases to identify a murderer. In the film *Fiddler on the Roof*, Tevye recounts a wild and scary dream in which the late wife of the butcher promises to haunt her former husband if he remarries. Tevye makes up the entire dream so that his wife, Golde, will agree to breaking up the contract for their daughter, Tzeitel, to marry the butcher in an arranged match. Tevye knows that claiming the message came to him in a dream will convince Golde. Tzeitel can then marry Motel, the man she loves.[32]

In *The Encyclopedia of Ghosts and Spirits*, author Rosemary Ellen Guiley notes that "encountering the dead in dreams is seen as the most powerful way a person can relate to sacred powers."[33] Trances work equally well as vehicles for precognitive experiences. Tribal shamans chant, dance, and take hallucinogenic drugs such as peyote to transport them into the spirit world.[34] The Muslim Sufis (sometimes called whirling dervishes) spin like tops to achieve trance and become one with Allah at the center of their spinning. Dances accompanied by sacred drums put practitioners of vodoun (the correct word for "voodoo") not only in trance but open to possession by their gods.

Trances, possessions, and raptures all qualify as altered states of consciousness, situations during which brain activity is either faster or slower, affecting response. Sleep is an altered state, usually defined by whether or not the sleeper is dreaming. In so-called **ganzfield**

(German for "entire space") simulations, test subjects stare at a large blank field of white and attempt to receive the telepathic messages of a sender. In experiments conducted in 1973 by Charles Honorton and S. Harper at Maimonides Hospital in New York, the meditative state achieved by staring at the white Ganzfield substantially increased psi ability. Nearly half the test subjects exhibited psi.[35]

PSYCHOKINESIS

Literally "mind over matter," psychokinesis can manifest itself either spontaneously or deliberately. Although sometimes associated with poltergeist phenomena, any change caused by thought alone is psychokinetic, such as passing hands over someone for healing; levitation; concentrating on coins landing a certain way or dice showing winning numbers; or, most dramatic, table-tipping, producing ectoplasm, or causing furniture and other objects to sail across the room. Calling forth a spirit or apparition in séance is a form of PK as well.

Pioneer psi researcher J. B. Rhine began studying PK in 1934 with a gambler that claimed he could influence dice to roll in his favor. Rhine was startled to find early test results in favor of the gambler's assertion, but success declined as the tests went on. Rhine concluded that PK and ESP were linked but were not subject to brain processes or the mechanical laws of physics.[36]

In the 1960s, physicist Helmut Schmidt conducted tests on "micro-PK" using an electronic coin flipper to see if subjects could affect whether a coin landed on heads or tails. Micro-PK refers to weaker or smaller changes in outcome that are not always seen with the naked eye. Schmidt's coin-flipping machine operated on the random decay of radioactive particles, and the process is not subject to outside forces. Schmidt asked volunteers to exert psi influence on the outcome. A few of the participants were somewhat successful. The coin flipper was the prototype for later random-event generators, tasks now handled by computers.

Meanwhile, research on "macro-PK," or larger-scale PK events that are easily seen, focused on spoon bending and other feats practiced by Israeli psychic Uri Geller. His television appearances were so intense that some viewers claimed the silverware in their kitchen drawers bent in sympathy with the Geller flatware.[37]

Some of the most intriguing research is in "retro-PK" or attempts to alter events that have already occurred, such as changing a string of numbers previously generated.[38] In Palo Alto, California, psychologist William Braud is studying the possibility of retro-PK as a means to go back in time and provide therapy for psychological behaviors before they turn into bigger problems or serious disorders.[39]

In the 1970s, PK researchers studied psychics and mediums to see whether their psi abilities could exert influence on stationary items. New York psychic Ingo Swann successfully changed the temperature of objects and influenced their magnetic fields as measured by a magnetometer. Sometimes temperature changes continued even after the test subject had finished, causing what scientists dubbed the "linger effect."[40]

SUPER-PSI

Super-psi (formerly known as *super-ESP*) refers to beefed-up psi or the limitless expansion of psi abilities. The enormity of such a proposition excites those who are trying to prove survival of the spirit. Research conducted as early as the 1920s, however, indicated that instead of receiving communications from the spirit world, psychics may have been relying on clairvoyance and extensive telepathy.

In a 1925 case, Dr. S. G. Soal asked London psychic Blanche Cooper if she could contact his friend Gordon Davis, believed killed in World War I. Cooper supposedly reached Davis, who talked about his wife and family through the medium. She even went so far as to use Davis' manner of speech. But the whole time, Davis was alive and living in London! Shocked, Soal felt Cooper had telepathically gleaned information about his friend from Soal's own mind.[41]

Telepathy and clairvoyance don't provide all the answers, however; supporters of super-psi cannot explain the presence of spirit "passers-by" who are not related to the subject or the psychic but choose to interrupt a reading, providing extraneous information. If telepathy and clairvoyance were the only options, apparitions would probably not manifest either, since a person who senses or sees a presence may not know that spirit. Very young children who tell remarkably detailed accounts of past lives previously unknown to anyone don't fit into the super-psi model either.[42]

Tools of the Trade

In *The Exorcist* (1973)—perhaps the scariest movie ever made—12-year-old Regan MacNeil (Linda Blair), left to amuse herself, finds a dusty old Ouija board in a closet of the house that she and her actress mother, Chris (Ellen Burstyn), are sharing in Georgetown, an upper-class neighborhood of Washington, D.C. One evening Chris offers to play the Ouija board with Regan, but the child replies that she has been playing alone with the board for quite some time, communicating with "Captain Howdy," and that Captain Howdy doesn't want Chris to play. Chris doesn't give Captain Howdy much thought initially. The friendly, children's-puppet-show nature of the spirit's name belies his evil nature, but in fact Captain Howdy is a demon. Once the demon possesses Regan and turns her into a hideous monster, spewing green slime, however, Chris is convinced that nothing short of a full exorcism can save the girl.[43]

PSYCHIC METHODS

The movie is based on a 1971 novel of the same name by William Peter Blatty, who in turn based his book on the account of a young boy's alleged possession and exorcism in Maryland in 1949. The story is a cautionary tale, and one of its messages is clear: Playing with a *talking board* or *planchette* device, such as a Ouija board, might be inviting trouble.

Ouija, a combination of the French "oui" and the German "ja" (both meaning yes), is the trade name for a Parker Brothers toy consisting of a game board illustrating the alphabet, the numerals 0 to 9, the words yes and no, and a planchette, or pointer, that slides over the board to indicate letters or numbers in answer to the players' questions. A planchette (French for "little board") can be anything that glides smoothly over the board, but in the Parker Brothers game it is a heart-shaped plastic piece on three legs.

Ouija boards were invented in 1892 by Elijah J. Bond. Bond sold his patent to William Fuld and his Baltimore Talking Board Company not long thereafter. Many homes had a Ouija board during and after World War I, when the loss of so many lives caused a resurgence of Spiritualism. Fuld manufactured the boards until 1966, when he sold the rights to Parker Brothers. The company unequivocally describes the boards as toys.[44] For a professional psychic, however, the Ouija board is no game. It is only one of many choices available to facilitate a reading, and when used by anyone other than a competent psychic, it poses a spiritual risk.

In ancient times—and even now within older cultural traditions—seers practiced the arts of *augury* (finding guidance in the flights of birds); *haruspicy* (reading the markings on animal entrails, particularly the liver); throwing bones, coins, or shells on a diagram and interpreting the results (a part of Santeria and vodoun worship going back to native African religions); knowing the meanings associated with swirling smoke or billowing clouds; and seeing visions after ingesting drugs or chemicals. In ancient Egypt, members of a cult that worshipped a sacred bull believed that the direction the bull turned in his stall provided answers to their questions.

Modern psychics may not consult bulls, but many of their preferred methods are not exactly new:

Astrology

A study of the positions of stars and planets in the heavens in the belief that the various alignments of the celestial bodies can influence

Figure 3.1 *A planchette device or Ouija board is a popular means of contacting the spirit world.* (Rainer Holz/zefa/Corbis)

personality and have a profound effect on individual actions and national decisions. The Chaldeans (Iraqis) and Babylonians (Iranians) developed a system in about 3000 BCE for mapping the stars' locations. The Egyptians started about 100 years earlier.

The ancient Greeks refined the system, correlating the 12 constellations through which the sun, moon, and planets travel each year with the activities associated with each star sign. The word *zodiac*, which means "circus of animals," also came from the Greeks.[45] The star signs and the portions of the year they supposedly influence are as follows (the year begins in the spring, when winter's deadness gives way to new life):

○ **Aries** (the ram): March 21–April 20

○ **Taurus** (the bull): April 21–May 21

○ **Gemini** (the twins): May 22–June 21

○ **Cancer** (the crab): June 22–July 23

○ **Leo** (the lion): July 24–August 23

○ **Virgo** (the virgin): August 24–September 23

○ **Libra** (the scales): September 24–October 23

○ **Scorpio** (the scorpion): October 24–November 22

○ **Sagittarius** (the centaur archer): November 23–December 22

○ **Capricorn** (the goat): December 23–January 20

○ **Aquarius** (the water bearer): January 21–February 19

○ **Pisces** (the fish): February 20–March 20

Chinese astrology also utilizes 12 animals, but each animal represents an entire lunar year, not one month. The Chinese astrological cycle, along with the character traits associated with each animal, is[46]

○ **Rat:** smart, successful, willing to make money

○ **Ox:** honest, patient, hard-working, poor communicator

○ **Tiger:** fierce, tolerant, loyal, courageous

○ **Rabbit:** gentle, sensitive, modest, merciful, long memory

○ **Dragon:** lively, energetic, fortunate, a leader

Figure 3.2 *This woodcut from a Medieval calendar depicts the signs of the Zodiac.* (Bettmann/Corbis)

- **Snake:** malevolent, catty, jealous, suspicious, psychic
- **Horse:** ingenious, wants to be in the limelight, clever, kind, active
- **Sheep (also Goat):** leader, polite, clever, kind-hearted
- **Monkey:** lively, flexible, creative, versatile, loves sports
- **Rooster:** honest, bright, punctual, warm-hearted, may be arrogant
- **Dog:** steadfast, faithful, courageous, warm-hearted
- **Pig:** honest, frank, calm, impatient, tolerant, optimistic

The Chinese system is a 12-year cycle. For example, the years of the Rat include 1948, 1960, 1972, 1984, and 1996. The years of the Ox

Figure 3.3 *A contemporary rendering of the signs of the Zodiac shows the signs have changed little over the years.* (Denis Scott/Corbis)

are 1949, 1961, 1973, 1985, and 1997. A complete 12-year cycle would add 12 years to those of each animal. Hence the next year of the Rat is 2008, the next year of the Ox is 2009, the next year of the Tiger is 2010, and so on. Chinese New Year can occur from late January to mid-February. If a birthday falls before New Year, it is considered part of the previous year.

Automatic writing

A spontaneous outpouring of written messages that flow unbidden through the hand and pen of a psychic; also called "inspired" writing. The psychic might be in a trance state or totally awake. Previously thought to be solely "bulletins from the beyond," examples of automatic writing now also include any psychically received knowledge.

Cards

Psychic readings with cards are one of the most popular methods of revealing the answers to a sitter's questions. The psychic reader shuffles and cuts the deck—or asks the sitter to perform that task—then lays out the cards in patterns called *spreads*. The reader can choose from thousands of spreads, but the Celtic Cross is a favorite pattern. One common and popular set of Tarot cards is the 1910 Rider-Waite deck.[47] (See Story of the Tarot on page 41.)

Choose a table cover that you will use only for the card turnings to establish its psychic connection to the cards, and keep the deck in its own special box, preferably wrapped in a silky, colorful fabric (red is

Figure 3.4 *This classically styled Tarot card shows Death.* (Bettmann/ Corbis)

Figure 3.5 *Fortune-tellers use different configurations of Tarot cards in their readings.* (Floris Leeuwenberg/The Cover Story/Corbis)

a good choice; black is not) within the box so that the cards are protected from bad influences.

Crystals

Casting crystals is much like tossing bones. In her book *The Complete Guide to Psychic Development*, Cassandra Eason advises putting together a bag of crystals or stones in the colors listed below, which represent certain properties:[48]

- **white:** for new beginnings, new ventures; quartz or moonstone
- **black:** for letting go of sorrow, grief or guilt, for acceptance, for the end of one period and the beginning of another; hematite, jet, obsidian or onyx

Story of the Tarot

A deck of cards: able to create or destroy fortunes, incite passion and anger, and maybe even cause death. And if the deck is a set of Tarot cards, the interpretation of the strange illustrations and symbols might also reveal psychic truths or give a glimpse into the future.

The oldest evidence of any type of playing card goes back only about 650 years to the fourteenth century. According to the *Encyclopedia of the Strange, Mystical and Unexplained,* the first cards that could be described as Tarot were created in 1392 by a painter named Jacquemin Gringonneur for King Charles VI of France. The word *tarot* is probably a French version of the Italian *tarocchi,* which means "triumphs" or "trumps."

In the fifteenth century, cards specified as Tarot were designed by Bonifacio Bembo[49] for members of the Visconti and Visconti-Sforza families, who ruled the city of Milan in Italy. These early decks encompassed what are now called the Major Arcana ("greater

Figure 3.6 *A Tarot card, by Bonifacio Bembo, depicts a knight.* (Gianni Dagli Orti/Corbis)

(continues)

(continued)

secrets"): 22 face cards with images representing symbols for death, fortune, power, the spirit, anger, love, wisdom, the sciences, and so forth. Dabblers in the occult tried to establish legends about the cards that would give them an older pedigree. An eighteenth century French archeologist and Egyptologist Antoine Court de Gebelin claimed the cards symbolized bits of ancient wisdom from the mythical *Book of Thoth,* while Eliphas Lévi, a nineteenth century French occultist, believed the cards corresponded to the Kabbalah, a Jewish mystical tradition.

Card games were extremely popular in Europe, and by the mid-eighteenth century Tarot decks had merged with regular suit cards to form what is known as a "Marseilles" deck: 78 cards composed of the 22 Major Arcana cards and 56 cards in the Minor Arcana ("lesser secrets"). The Minor Arcana has four suits—pentacles (diamonds), wands (clubs), swords (spades), and cups (hearts)—and each suit has four "court" cards: king, queen, jack, and page (only Tarot decks have page cards). In general, the swords indicate bad luck, the pentacles symbolize wealth and success, the cups reveal good luck and love, and the wands stand for successful ventures and rewards for distinction and service.

In 1910, Englishman Arthur Edward Waite, a member of the Hermetic Order of the Golden Dawn (a group of leading social and literary figures dedicated to the study of the occult), worked with fellow Order member Pamela Colman Smith to design and illustrate a Tarot deck that represented what he felt was the ancient symbolism of the cards.[50] Their collaboration, which came to be known as the Rider-Waite deck, set the standard. Smith even illustrated the "pip" cards (the numbered cards in each suit); her drawings for the cards in both the Major and Minor Arcana are bright and colorful but vaguely hypnotic and mysterious.

It may be the cards's strange beauty that makes them so appealing.

○ **brown:** for practical matters, home and finances, animals, order; tigereye, chrysoberyl, amber, smoky quartz, petrified wood, banded agate

○ **pink:** for family, children, reconciliation, care of others; pink coral, rhodonite, rhodochrosite, rose quartz, sodalite, pink kunzite, pink mother of pearl

○ **red:** for courage, challenge, passion, fertility, anger, positive change; garnet, carnelian, red jasper, blood agate, red calcite

○ **orange:** for identity, happiness, health, rivalries, balance, partnerships, equality; orange amber, orange carnelian, citrine, jasper, orange quartz, orange beryl

○ **yellow:** for communication, undeveloped potential, logic and learning, interviews, the sun; yellow citrine, zircon, topaz, golden amber, beryl, yellow quartz

○ **green:** for love, romance, sympathy, friendship, intuition; emerald, malachite, aventurine, peridot, jade, green zircon, moss agate

○ **blue:** for matters of principle, justice, altruism, worldly affairs, career; turquoise, blue howlite, azurite, lapis lazuli, labradorite

○ **purple:** for healing of the soul and spirit, wisdom, religious insight, psychic development; sodalite, sugilite, amethyst, purple fluorite, lilac kunzite

Some crystals, such as amethyst, carnelian, black and red jasper, garnet, lapis lazuli, tigereye, and topaz, also protect the psychic from negative energy. Protection crystals must be washed frequently in running water to cleanse them of the negative energies they absorb. If the crystals have come into contact with very bad influences, sprinkle salt on the stones after cleaning; purify them with incense and the flame of a purple, silver, or pink candle; and let them rest in a dark cloth for a few days to re-energize.[51]

Figure 3.7 *A crystal ball like those used by some psychics.* (Pascal Deloche/ Godong/Corbis)

Dowsing

An ancient skill used to find water, minerals, or oil deposits beneath the earth, probably related to the confluence of psychic and geomagnetic forces. The word "dowser" may come from the Middle English term *duschen*, meaning "to strike," or from the Old Cornish words *dewys* ("goddess") and *rhodl* ("tree branch"). Dowsers traditionally use a Y-shaped tree branch, holding onto the "Y" while walking over a piece of ground and occasionally striking the soil with the limb. When water or other deposits are detected, the branch shakes and appears to point down to the right spot. Dowsing can be used to find lost objects, money, pets, ghosts, and people, live or dead.[52]

Dreams

Long considered to be the doorway to another realm, dreams may guide the psychic into a better understanding of the messages received. In more traditional cultures, dreams are vital to the connections between the worlds of known existence and those of the spirit. The aboriginal peoples of Australasia (Australia, New Zealand, and nearby Pacific isles) refer to the land of their creation, as well as its manifestation, as Dreamtime. Native American peoples make dreamcatchers, circular forms criss-crossed with leather strips and decorated with beads and feathers, in order to catch and keep dreams.

The Greek philosopher Aristotle said of dreams and dreamers that anyone could interpret dreams that were vivid, but those with great skill were able to explain what he called the "resemblances," or cor-relations between the dream's images and waking life.[53]

(For more discussion of psychic dreaming, see Chapter Two.)

Herbs and Tea Leaves

Interpreting the patterns of herbs or tea leaves that remain in a cup or plate after the liquid has been poured off. Using tea leaves or herbs to facilitate psychic readings is an old practice, principally because the plants were available and plentiful to anyone.

I Ching

Ancient Chinese philosophy in which the questioner tosses three coins three times, forming patterns interpreted by looking inside oneself for enlightenment. Emperor Fu-hsi supposedly devised the original hexagram patterns, formed from two trigrams, about 2850 BCE. The hexagrams were drawn with solid lines, representing the active, male force of *yang*, and broken lines, representing the passive, female force of *yin*.

Both Lao-tzu, founder of Taoism, and the teacher Confucius stud-ied and interpreted the *I Ching*. The psychiatrist Carl Jung used the *I Ching* as a model of what he called synchronicity: the relation between the random coin tosses and their outcomes.[54]

Palms

Reading the lines on a human palm, called *palmistry* or *chiromancy*, probably dates back over four thousand years. Palmistry reached its peak during the Middle Ages but was forced underground in the 1400s when the Church forbade the practice. Prior to that time, Scripture seemed to support palm reading: "Length of days in her right hand, and in her left hand riches and honor." (Proverbs 3:16).

A palm reader first examines the shape of the sitter's hand, then looks at the left hand for indications of destiny at birth and then the right to see if the sitter's destiny is being realized. The readings are reversed for left-handed people. Palmistry remains popular in China, where acupuncturists believe that the lines of a palm indicate changes in the body's internal organs.[55]

Planchettes

Planchettes or talking boards were used in ancient Greece as far back as 540 BCE. Although the devices were extremely popular in the years between the wars, they languished until the 1960s and 1970s, when interest in the New Age resurfaced.

In 1963 poet and author Jane Roberts began channeling a spirit named Seth who had contacted Jane through her board. Although Jane maintained Seth was perfectly harmless, others did not classify Seth as benign.[56]

Psychometry

Using an object to sense impressions either about the object itself or the object's owner or user. Psychic detectives usually ask for a personal item to obtain the best profile. However, a flower selected at random by the sitter from a mixed bouquet can also provide the reader with information about that person's personality and character.[57]

Scrying

Peering into objects or liquids with smooth, reflective surfaces to see psychic images. The word "scry" is English, probably a derivative of *descry*: "to make out dimly." It is sometimes pronounced as "shreeing."

In *The Wizard of Oz*, the Wicked Witch of the West has an enormous crystal ball in which she watches Dorothy (Judy Garland). The wizards in *Lord of the Rings* depend on the power of the *palantíri*, the crystal orbs that show places and events far away in space and time and that could communicate with each other.[58] Professor Dumbledore in the Harry Potter books owns a Pensieve: a basin of water that not only shows images of the past, present, and future but accepts retrieved memories that enter the water's pictures as wisps of smoke. And in the novel *Jonathan Strange and Mr. Norrell*, magician Jonathan Strange produces images in pools of water or wine spilled directly onto his hosts' dinner tables.[59] The most famous magic mirror might be the one owned by the Wicked Queen in *Snow White*; nearly any child can recite "Mirror, mirror on the wall, who's the fairest one of all?"

Psychics Through the Ages

The Renaissance introduced Western Europe to new ideas about art, literature, science, and man's place in God's universe, but rulers and powerful leaders in the Roman Catholic Church clung to old beliefs and threatened retribution against anyone who disagreed.

In France, physician Michel de Nostradame, better known as Nostradamus (the Latin form of his name), began experiencing prophetic visions in the mid-1500s. Afraid of censure or worse from the Inquisition, Nostradamus retired to a small, relatively secret room in his home where he gazed into a bowl of water set upon a bronze tripod and witnessed horrible images of war and destruction to come through the ages. Although Nostradamus published his accounts of these revelations, he purposely obscured them by combining French, Latin, Italian, Greek, and the Provençal dialect within the verses, even using anagrams.[60]

Supporters credit Nostradamus with predicting the French Revolution; the rise and fall of Napoleon Bonaparte; the Great Fire of London in 1666; Adolf Hitler and World War II; the assassination of President John F. Kennedy; and the coming of a third Antichrist and World War III (Bonaparte and Hitler are Antichrists one and two). [61]

Nostradamus' most ardent fans even believe he foresaw the September 11, 2001, terrorist attacks on New York, referred to as the "new city," but the vagueness of the real translations and the circulation of bogus verses make that prediction doubtful.[62]

Figure 4.1 *Many people consider Michel Nostradamus, seen here in a French engraving, to have been a prophet who predicted wars, assassinations, and other terrible events centuries before they occurred.* (Stefano Bianchetti/CORBIS)

Nostradamus denied being a prophet. But if one compares what he wrote more than 450 years ago with actual events, the alleged similarities are rather creepy. Nevertheless, many of Nostradamus' pronouncements have been stretched to the limits of credibility to fit events that happened hundreds of years after he wrote them. His most famous work, *The Prophecies* (also spelled *Profities*), has remained in print since his death: a three-volume collection of four-line verses called *quatrains* organized in groups of 100. Each 100-quatrain group is a *centurie:* a convenient means of sorting the quatrains, added after Nostradamus' death in 1566, which has no connection to 100-year periods. Nostradamus did not complete his project as intended, for he had planned 10 volumes containing 10 centuries of quatrains, or 1,000 prophecies. The three books were published in 1555, 1557, and 1558, but the last book survives only as part of a combined edition published posthumously in 1568. All together there are 941 rhymed quatrains and one that doesn't rhyme for a total of 942.[63]

The following quatrain, translated into English, reputedly refers to Napoleon Bonaparte:

> *An Emperor shall be born near Italy*
> *Who shall cost the Empire dear.*

They shall say, with what people he keeps company
He shall be found less a Prince than a butcher.

Centurie I, quatrain 60

Napoleon was born on the island of Corsica, off Italy, and did not limit his acquaintances to members of the upper classes. Regarding Hitler,[64] Nostradamus reportedly prophesied:

Beasts ferocious with hunger will cross the rivers,
The greater part of the battlefield will be against Hister.
Into a cage of iron will the great one be drawn,
When the child of Germany observes nothing.

Centurie II, quatrain 24

Although "Hister" is usually interpreted as Nostradamus' so-close approximation of "Hitler," the Danube River was known as Hister in the sixteenth century.[65]

The study of Nostradamus has practically become an industry, with books, films, and even songs being published and produced year after year. But Nostradamus was not the only person in history said to possess the gift of precognition.

EMANUEL SWEDENBORG (1688–1772)

Like Nostradamus, Swedenborg practiced medicine; before that he was special assessor to the Swedish Royal College of Mines.[66] In 1743, at age 56, Swedenborg began having detailed visions in which he traveled to Heaven and Hell and other spiritual planes. He experienced vivid dreams, ecstatic visions, trances, spirit communications, and even conversations with God and angels. Swedenborg claimed that God had named him a spiritual emissary to bring the truth of the afterlife to an ignorant mankind.

Figure 4.2 *Swedish mystic Emanuel Swedenborg is known for, among other things, his vivid account of the nature of Hell.* (Bettmann/CORBIS)

Swedenborg relinquished other pursuits to fulfill his mission. He published the first book of a ponderous eight-volume series entitled *Arcana Coelestia* ("celestial secrets") in 1749. Through 14 more books over the next 25 years, Swedenborg continued to write about his experiences with God and the angels, describing the afterlife, its habits, structures and inhabitants (see Heaven and Hell According to Swedenborg and Browne on page 62) in spectacular detail.

Swedenborg also gained fame as a clairvoyant and remote viewer, credited with witnessing a 1759 fire in Stockholm even though he was at a dinner party 300 miles away. The philosopher Immanuel Kant, who confirmed this event, was initially impressed with Swedenborg, but in later years Kant decided Swedenborg was insane and should be incarcerated.[67] Swedenborg spent his latter years in England, preaching his vision of man's simultaneous existence in the parallel worlds of the natural and the "inner domain" of the spirit. His work built the foundation for much of today's New Age practice.[68]

EDGAR CAYCE (1877–1945)

Perhaps seen as a man unlikely to exhibit paranormal powers, Cayce was one of the most successful healers and remote viewers of all time. His ability to describe the problem within a patient, even from great distance, and then prescribe medicines and health regimens for a cure baffled trained physicians and researchers.

Cayce showed psychic ability in boyhood, but his powers were generally ignored. By his early 20s, the laryngitis and persistent cough that Cayce had suffered for years had cost him his job as a salesman. In desperation he turned to hypnotist Al Layne. While Cayce was in a trance state, Layne asked him to describe his affliction and suggest a cure. Cayce diagnosed his own cough, and when he returned to full consciousness his voice had returned. Cayce began giving readings and healings in 1901.

Cayce was accurate approximately 90 percent of the time, and word of his astounding successes spread quickly. Distance between Cayce and a patient was immaterial, as he was a remote viewer. His method consisted of lying down and becoming as relaxed as possible, at which time he would lose consciousness and visualize all of the body's tissues, organs, nerves, blood vessels, and even the tiniest cells, which would then reveal their illness to Cayce. His diagnoses were based on more than just symptoms and took into account childhood sickness and accidents, glandular conditions, hereditary disorders, and other factors. Healing progressed faster if the patient expressed a positive attitude. Cayce claimed that psychic vibrations were everywhere and available to everyone; at peak, psychokinetic energy results.

Figure 4.3 *Prophet and psychic Edgar Cayce is said to have possessed great healing powers.* (Bettmann/ CORBIS)

By 1911 Cayce had become convinced that *karma*—the idea that what one suffers in this life is a means of atoning for or working out the mistakes made in another life—was a cause of physical illness.[69] He studied reincarnation and became convinced that he had been an ancient Egyptian priest practicing medicine more than 10,000 years ago, among other lives. Cayce advocated bringing the body into equilibrium through natural healing. In 1931, Cayce founded the Association for Research and Enlightenment (ARE) in Virginia Beach, Virginia to promote and support his work.[70]

LEONORA EVELINA SIMONDS PIPER (1859–1950)

One of the greatest mental mediums of all time, Mrs. Piper stumped many skeptics who expected to see a conjurer and came away amazed at her accuracy.

Leonora had her first psychic experience at age eight when an unseen presence slapped her right ear and said, "Aunt Sara, not dead, but with you still."

Mrs. Piper's most important supporter was philosopher William James, who was so impressed with her powers that he became her first manager and secured rights to arrange sittings. James was referring to Mrs. Piper when he famously asserted that if you wanted to prove that not all crows are black, you only have to find one white one.[71]

After managing Mrs. Piper for two years, James turned the responsibility over to Richard Hodgson, new head of the American Society for Psychical Research (ASPR). Mrs. Piper amazed Hodgson as well, and he arranged for an English tour in 1889. Through 1890 Mrs. Piper gave 83 sittings, all with astonishing accuracy. Her spirit control, the French doctor Phinuit (pronounced "Finney"), was rather unreliable, but through him Mrs. Piper gave the most convincing evidence of spirit survival that critics had ever experienced.

When Hodgson died in 1905, her management passed to James Hyslop, who arranged a second English tour in 1906. Unfortunately, Mrs. Piper's sittings after her return were handled poorly, and she was harshly treated during testing of her powers under trance. She made a third trip to England in 1909–1911, but the earlier abuse caused Mrs. Piper to suffer temporary loss of her gift. She could communicate via automatic writing but lost her trance abilities.

Prior to the discovery of Mrs. Piper, psi research had concentrated on physical mediumship and what phenomena could be produced as proof. From Mrs. Piper's day onward, the emphasis has been to understand mental mediumship, and that is her greatest legacy.[72]

JEANE DIXON
(1918–1997)

Dixon may have been the most recognizable psychic of the mid-twentieth century, writing a syndicated daily astrology column, consulting with political figures, publishing books, and making television appearances. During World War II, Jeane gave readings to servicemen and government officials, including President Franklin D. Roosevelt.

Dixon claimed to have predicted the assassination of Mahatma Gandhi; the airplane deaths of actress Carole Lombard and the United Nation's second Secretary-General Dag Hammarskjöld; the suicide of Marilyn

Figure 4.4 *Well-known psychic Jeane Dixon claimed to have predicted the assassination of John F. Kennedy.* (Solters/Roskin/Friedman, Inc.)

In Your Dreams

As discussed in Chapter Two, many cultures place great value on dreams, believing they can serve as "paranormal e-mail" between the living and those who have passed. One's background may influence dream interpretation; in Iranian lore, good dreams are kept secret, much like wishes over birthday candles, or they won't come true.

In the classic book *Extraordinary Popular Delusions and the Madness of Crowds,* author Charles Mackay denies the possibility of spirit communication in dreams, noting sarcastically that "it is not uncommon to find the members of a family regularly every morning narrating their dreams at the breakfast-table, and becoming happy or miserable for the day according to their interpretation."[73]

Dreaming of trees, apparently, is especially revealing. To the superstitious, dreams of ash trees signify long journeys, while those of lime trees send the sleeping traveler across the ocean. Yews and alders mean sickness or death. Mackay comments wryly that every plant that grows probably symbolizes good or evil for someone.

To recognize the significance of the images imbedded in a nocturnal garden, here is a partial list of fruits, flowers, and vegetables and what they meant in Mackay's day:[74]

- **asparagus:** if tied in bundles, tears; if seen growing, it means good fortune
- **aloe:** if without a flower, long life; with a flower, a legacy
- **artichoke:** signifies receipt of a favor from a person you'd least expect
- **agrimony:** an herb indicating sickness in the home
- **anemone:** love

- **auriculas:** good luck planted in beds; in pots, marriage; if gathered, widowhood
- **bilberries:** indicate a pleasant excursion
- **broom flowers:** an increase in family size
- **cauliflower:** either all your friends will slight you, or you will suddenly become poor and none of your friends will care
- **daffodil:** maidens who dream of daffodils should take care not to go with their lovers into the woods or any dark or hidden place for their screams might not be heard
- **fig:** if green, embarrassment; if dried, money to the poor and laughter to the rich
- **heart's-ease:** the pain of a broken heart
- **lemon:** a separation
- **lily:** joy
- **pomegranate:** happiness to newlyweds; reconciliation to warring partners
- **quince:** pleasant company will visit
- **rose:** happy love unmixed with sorrow
- **sorrel:** a calamity could soon befall you if you are not very cautious
- **sunflower:** your pride will suffer
- **violet:** predict joy to married folks and evil to single ones
- **water lily:** danger from the sea
- **yellow flowers (of any kind):** jealousy
- **yew berries:** loss of character (reputation) for a person of either sex

Monroe; China's embrace of Communism; the partition of India into that nation and Pakistan; and the Soviet Union's launch of the first space capsule, Sputnik.[75]

But by far Dixon's most famous prognostication was reported in a May 1956 issue of the Sunday newspaper magazine *Parade*. In that article, Dixon wrote that the 1960 presidential election would be dominated by labor issues and won by a Democrat, whom she described as tall, young, brown-haired, and blue-eyed. She went on to say that this president would be assassinated or die in office but not necessarily in his first term.[76]

Her loyal public remembered her hits and overlooked her misses, a tendency called the "Jeane Dixon effect" by Temple University mathematician John Allen Paulos.

5

Psychic Nation:
The Paranormal Is With Us

A stargate is a ring-shaped portal or device that is part of a system of similar portals throughout the universe, allowing teleportation to other worlds and other planetary civilizations that are light years apart, at least in science fiction novels and television shows. Yet the story that such passageways are "military secrets" may not be too far from the truth. For years the U.S. government sponsored a top-secret operation called Star Gate to utilize **remote viewing**, the ability to perceive events, places, or people without regard to space, time, distance, or circumstances. In other words, the U.S. military used psychics, proving again that truth is stranger than fiction.

REMOTE VIEWING

One of the oldest expressions of psi, remote viewing has been practiced for centuries by shamans and ordinary individuals alike. Remote viewers either "see" with their psychic second sight or mentally travel in an out-of-body experience to psychically look more closely. Originally called traveling clairvoyance or telesthesia, the ability was dubbed remote viewing by physicists and researchers Russell Targ and Harold Puthoff. Targ suggested that the more accurate terminology might be remote sensing, because all the senses could be involved in the experience.[77]

The Greek historian Herodotus wrote what might be the first account of remote viewing when he reported on the tests of psychic power administered by King Croesus of Lydia in 550 BCE. The King sent out messengers to seven oracles and asked each to "see" what His Majesty was doing that day. Pythia, oracle of Apollo at Delphi, was the winner. She could see King Croesus himself preparing a stew in a brass-lidded cauldron and could smell the lamb and tortoise boiling in the pot.[78]

Other remote viewers include Emanual Swedenborg and Edgar Cayce (see Chapter Four), the military's cadre of psychic spies, those involved in psychic criminology or archaeology, or anyone who has ever described a previously unknown place or event in great detail. In the nineteenth century, Frederic W. H. Myers, one of the founders of the Society for Psychical Research, observed that remote viewing seemed to be part clairvoyance and telepathy with precognition and retrocognition.[79]

At SRI International (formerly the Stanford Research Institute) in California, Targ and Puthoff began studying remote viewing in 1972 and collected data for at least 10 years. They established protocols requiring a "double-blind" set-up of at least two people present—the viewer and another—and neither of them can have any knowledge of the target object or situation[80] so that no information is unethically gained or shared. After collecting reams of data, Targ and Puthoff concluded that remote viewing was not only possible and practical but that anyone could be trained to do it.

Army Intelligence Officer Joseph McMoneagle (1946–), known as Viewer 001, was part of a special unit that provided psychic information to such agencies as the Central Intelligence Agency; the Defense Intelligence Agency; the Secret Service; the National Security Agency; the National Security Council; the FBI; the Drug Enforcement Agency; the U.S. Coast Guard; the State Department; the Department of Defense; the Bureau of Alcohol, Tobacco, and Firearms; and other classified organizations for more than 18 years.[82] Ingo Swann, the psychic who could alter an object's temperature (see Chapter Two), used remote viewing to guide a submarine to the unidentified site of a shipwreck. Swann claimed he could see anywhere on the globe if given the latitude and longitude.[83] Dean Radin also served as a remote viewer for the government.

In 1980, parapsychologist Stephan A. Schwartz of The Mobius Group, a consulting firm Schwartz founded in 1977, demonstrated the superiority of remote viewing over sophisticated sonar equipment in an archaeological search for the ancient sections of the city of Alexandria, Egypt. While the sonar revealed only one significant find, remote viewing uncovered several locations just as Schwartz had envisioned them—in particular, the ancient seawall, which extended 63 meters farther out than expected.[84]

But while these applications were fascinating, the experiments to gauge the success of remote viewing on buying silver futures were the most intriguing. As discussed in Chapter Two, using psi to buy and sell at just the right moment would be quite profitable if it worked.

In 1982 Targ and psychic Keith Harary conducted *associative remote viewing* tests, meaning that certain objects, viewed remotely, were used as surrogates for analytical data—in this case, the different price points for silver futures. A group of investors bought and sold the futures based on the objects Harary envisioned, such as a perfume vial, eyeglass frames, and a plastic bag filled with washers. Harary did not know which futures' prices corresponded to which objects. The investors originally pocketed more than $100,000, but their initial success didn't last.[85]

THE MODERN PSYCHICS

Spying, speculating in silver futures, or accompanying archaeologists to a dig do not exemplify the routines of most currently practicing psychics, however. What contemporary seers do have in common is enormous media access and savvy. They sell inspirational books, CDs, DVDs, and videotapes. They appear regularly on television chat shows and on talk radio. They provide private readings in person, over the telephone, or even on the Internet. A few of them produce or consult for their own television series. A handful have attained celebrity status.

Heaven and Hell According to Swedenborg and Browne

There may be about 250 years between the lives and works of Emanuel Swedenborg and Sylvia Browne, but their descriptions of Heaven and Hell are remarkably similar in some aspects. Both are fascinated with the organization of the Other Side.

Swedenborg describes three Heavens: the natural, the spiritual, and the celestial. These levels are distinct, and angels from each level cannot communicate.[87] Browne's Heaven is a mere three feet above the ground[88] and only one level, not three. Here, everyone speaks Aramaic.[89] Both agree that Heaven is quite beautiful, with mountains, valleys, seas, gardens, and plains. Browne says that the temperature is a constant 78° F.[90]

Most buildings in Browne's Heaven are in the Greco-Roman style, although many famous structures such as the Pyramids, the Sphinx, and the Taj Mahal are there, as are the fabled libraries of Alexandria, the Vatican, and Mecca.[91] Swedenborg describes cities with palaces and houses, businesses, books, gold and silver, and precious stones: everything to be found in the natural world but more perfect.[92] Browne's citizens live in houses, erected and decorated by projected thought alone.[93]

Swedenborg says there are two cities in Heaven that resemble London, and that most of the English live there. The roofed and gated streets of the Dutch district are designed to confuse and annoy nosy visitors so

Seeking consolation and confirmation from a psychic is both more common and less questionable than in years past. Robert Thompson, professor of media and popular culture at Syracuse University, notes that when faced with enormous and complicated issues, some people shun rational explanations and seek different answers.[86]

Following are descriptions of some of the most popular prognosticators and the media machine that supports them.

they won't interfere into Dutch business.[94] People have occupations and conduct business in Swedenborgian Heaven. In Browne's Heaven, money and trade do not exist.

Browne says there is no sex or need for marriage in Heaven. Swedenborg asserts that marriage and conjugal bliss are part of paradise.[95] Adultery, however, is not tolerated in Swedenborg's Heaven and guarantees a ticket to Hell.[96]

All residents of Swedenborgian Heaven are angels, except for young children, who become angels when they attain wisdom as adolescents.[97] Rich and poor alike are welcome. Hell has no demons or Satan, for those who choose lives of evil and self-love make their own misery. To Browne, angels are separate beings from humans.

Pets are a treasured group in Browne's Heaven. All kinds of animals, even those now extinct, live harmoniously in Heaven—all, that is, except insects. Her Heaven is bug free (although insect pets are presumably tolerated).[98]

For Browne, Hell is repudiation of God, a bleak nothingness. At death the spirit immediately passes through the Left Door and reincarnates. Browne says that residents from the Other Side may wait for hundreds of years, but if they're quick and grab that lost spirit before it passes through the Left Door it can be welcomed into God's unconditional heavenly love.[99] After all, Browne says confidently, when we are in Heaven, we are at Home. Believers choose when and if they will return.

SYLVIA BROWNE (1936–)

A practicing medium and psychic for more than 50 years, Browne enjoys a devoted following. Her inspirational books are such dependable bestsellers that two publishing houses—Dutton and Hay House—profitably share publication rights.[100]

Browne shares a birthday with psychic John Edward (October 19). She inherited her gift from her grandmother and has passed it down to her son and partner, Chris Dufresne, and his daughter, Angelia. Psi has existed in their family for more than 300 years.[101] Browne's spirit guide, Francine, often gives readings and lectures as herself.[102] With her books and TV and radio appearances, Browne is a psychic phenomenon in her own right.

JOHN EDWARD (1969–)

Born John Edward McGee, Edward pursued careers in dance instruction and medicine before finally giving into "the Boys" as he calls them—his spirit guides—and working as a full-time psychic.[103]

By 1995 Edward was giving readings full time and had written his first book, *One Last Time*. In 1998, Dr. Gary Schwartz, professor of clinical psychology and head of The Veritas Research Program at the University of Arizona, tested Edward's psychic ability at his research laboratory and pronounced Edward quite

Figure 5.1 *Psychic John Edward is the star of* John Edward Cross Country. *(Evan Agostini/Getty Images)*

talented. It wasn't until Edward got his own television show in 2000, *Crossing Over With John Edward*, that his career as a psychic really came together.

His popularity allows him to make TV appearances on talk shows, weekly news shows, and even comedies. His latest program is *John Edward Cross Country*, which debuted in 2006.[104]

JAMES VAN PRAAGH (1958–)

Raised a Catholic, Van Praagh often prayed for proof of God's existence, and at age eight his prayers were answered. Waking up to a cold gust of wind, he looked up and saw a huge hand, palm down, descending from the ceiling and radiating light. Unafraid, he took the vision as evidence of God's protection.[105] After considering the priesthood and working in broadcasting, a psychic told him he possessed the gift, and Van Praagh began studying mediumship and developing his intuition.[106]

Four spirits guide Van Praagh: Sister Theresa of the Order of the Sisters of Mercy; Master Chang, a Chinese gentleman; Harry Aldrich, an English physician; and Golden Feather, a Native American. Van Praagh began giving readings and teaching that each of us has the "God spark" within.[107]

Van Praagh is co-executive producer of the television program *Ghost Whisperer*, starring

Figure 5.2 *Psychic James Van Praagh is the co-executive producer of* Ghost Whisperer, *a television series loosely based on his real-life psychic experiences. (Gaas/AP)*

Jennifer Love Hewitt.[108] The plots of *Ghost Whisperer* are supposedly based on Van Praagh's psychic experiences.

ALLISON DUBOIS (1972–)

DuBois is the real-life inspiration for the TV series *Medium*, with most of the details of her life intact. Only her daughters' names have been changed to protect their identities. DuBois has worked for the Phoenix district attorney as a jury consultant. She calls herself a profiler, believing that "psychic" has negative connotations.

Figure 5.3 *Allison DuBois (right), inspiration for the TV series* Medium, *makes a public appearance with the show's executive producer Glen Gordon Caron (left) and actress Patricia Arquette (center).* (Nick Ut/AP)

Her first psychic experience occurred after her great-grandfather's funeral, when Allison was six. Her mom's disbelief in Allison's psychic gifts led her to deny them.[109]

DuBois' first missing-person case involved assisting the Texas Rangers in the search for a little girl, but she was unsuccessful.[110] DuBois takes particular interest in child safety and helped establish the Amber Alert system, which notifies the media about child abduction, in Arizona.[111]

DEREK ACORAH (1950–)

Probably Britain's most famous psychic working today, Acorah was the "resident psychic" from 2000–2005 on the television program *Most Haunted*, which appears in new and syndicated episodes internationally.

When a very young Derek reported seeing a man on the stairs later identified as his late grandfather, his grandmother pronounced the boy "the one."[112] He pursued a career in professional football (soccer) first but eventually began giving private readings and doing radio, TV, and live performances. Acorah's spirit guide, Sam, is a 2,000-year-old Ethiopian warrior.[113]

Acorah's role on the reality show *Most Haunted* was to channel the ghostly entities while an anthropologist, a parapsychologist, and a medical doctor explained the history of the site's inhabitants or ran from an apparition.[114]

LISA WILLIAMS (c. 1969–)

Although British psychic Williams had her first psi experience at age four, she didn't really pursue her gift until her 20s, after the death of her grandmother. She gave her first client reading at the age of 24 after practicing on her friends.

Psychic Detectives

In the early days of psychic showmanship, physical mediums proved their talent by showing off spirit-inspired writing or drawing, bringing forth a hairy hand, or causing tables to teeter tipsily. But as the world has grown more dangerous, a number of psychics have turned to crime-fighting to earn their stripes. Sylvia Browne, Allison DuBois, and Joe Mc-Moneagle all claim to be psychic detectives.

Perhaps foremost among the psychic detectives is Noreen Renier, who did not recognize her powers until late in her career. While working at Disney World in Orlando in 1976, she accompanied a friend to a reading and was intrigued by the psychic's accuracy. Renier began studying and practicing until she was a full-time psychic.[115]

Renier's specialty is *psychometry*, what British psychic Geraldine Cummins once called "memory divining."[116] To help provide additional leads to the police, especially in missing-person cases, Renier puts her hand on an object belonging to the victim and tries to visualize a location, time, or event that law enforcement personnel may not have considered. Then the detectives take over, following the tips.

Dr. William Roll, director of the Psychical Research Foundation, tested Renier and found her quite accurate. Renier has reportedly worked on several difficult cases involving rape, murder, missing persons, and plane crashes. Her most famous association was with Robert K. Ressler,

Her reality television program, *Lisa Williams: Life Among the Dead*, follows Williams as she sees clients or tries to explain weird phenomena in haunted locations. Williams—who dresses casually and sports two-color hair—projects a more relaxed approach than that of her peers who perform for a studio audience or on a talk show.

retired Special Agent for the FBI's Behavioral Science Unit in Quantico, Virginia, and one of the inspirations for *The Silence of the Lambs* and *The X Files.* Renier supposedly convinced Ressler of her ability when she predicted that President Ronald Reagan would be shot.[117] Jackie Peterson, mother of Scott Peterson, hired Renier to help find the body of her daughter-in-law, Laci, and clear her son's name. Unfortunately, Renier's conclusions implicated Scott, who was convicted of murdering his pregnant wife.[118]

In a documentary entitled *Medium: We See Dead People*, Pam Coronado was profiled as a psychic crime fighter. She described her visions about a crime or victim as "postcard moments."[119]

But do the psychics really advance a case, or are they an annoyance to police at best and a hindrance at worst? According to a fact sheet compiled by Dr. Dennis McFadden, psychology professor at the University of Texas at Austin, claiming to be a psychic sleuth gets the practitioner media attention and respectability.[120] In fact, according to excerpts from a 1992 book entitled *The Blue Sense: Psychic Detectives and Crime,* authors Arthur Lyons and Marcello Truzzi note that both the FBI and the National Center for Missing and Exploited Children deny that a psychic has ever solved a missing-person case.[121] Psychic Allison DuBois, who claims to have worked with the Texas Rangers, says that because working with psychics could open law enforcement officials to ridicule, the police usually deny all involvement.[122]

Williams claims she has met the spirits of Marilyn Monroe, Princess Diana, Natalie Wood, Ray Charles, and Bob Hope. When she makes contact with spirits, she first gets the chills, then sees "energy blobs of light" coming toward her. Nine times out of 10, she says spirits want to talk but perhaps not if they committed suicide.[123]

MAKING A CONNECTION

Some psychics work via telephone and the Internet, like Dionne Warwick's Psychic Friends Network. They charge a fee per minute for a reading. Some of these services offer the first few minutes free, but the reading usually takes longer, and charges quickly add up. Most of the advertisements for these psychics run late at night, attracting night-shift workers, insomniacs, and lonely souls looking for answers.

SUPERNATURAL APPEAL

It seems as if the public can't get enough of books, movies, radio, TV shows, or celebrity psychics. Whether one is a true believer or a skeptic, the possibility of getting a glimpse into the future or a message from the past can be a tremendous attraction. In the entertainment industry, a subject that remains eternally popular is called an *evergreen*, and books and shows about the unexplained definitely fall into that category.

What is the pull of the paranormal? Is it illusion? Kids of all ages love magic shows. J. K. Rowling, author of the wildly successful Harry Potter books, knows that part of Harry's appeal is fascination with his conjuring skills and his ability to put stuffy old Muggles in their places with a wave of his wand.

On the other hand, maybe the interest in psychic phenomena springs from fears of the dark or things that are creepy. The simple fact that years of testing, research, and anecdotal proof still haven't confirmed the reality of psi is in itself rather unsettling.

Whatever the reason, the supernatural is big business; weird stuff sells. Rowling is the first person to earn more than a billion dollars just for writing books—and she started her first book on a paper napkin!

Now that's magic.

Testing, Testing,
or Does Psi Really Exist?

In the 1984 film *Ghostbusters*, Dan Aykroyd, Bill Murray, and Harold Ramis play three parapsychology professors at Columbia University. As the movie opens, Dr. Peter Venkman (Murray) is administering a forced-card test to a pair of students, one male and one female. He turns over a card with a symbol on it, called a Zener card, without showing it to either student and encourages them to identify the symbol using psi. If either student guesses correctly, great; if not, the wrong guess elicits an electric zap. Venkman, trying to eliminate his competition so he can date the woman, zaps the man every time and claims the co-ed must be endowed with psychic powers.[124]

Dr. Venkman may have used the Zener cards for his own agenda, but such examinations are legitimate tests of psi. They were developed in the 1930s and 1940s by Joseph Banks Rhine—commonly called J. B.—as a means of scientifically proving what was then called extrasensory perception.

J. B. RHINE (1895–1980) AND
LOUISA E. RHINE (1891–1983)

Considered the father of modern psychic research,[125] Rhine was born in rural Pennsylvania. Surrounded by the stories and superstitions of

Figure 6.1 *Zener cards are a simple means of testing or developing psychic talent. Try it out by photocopying these pages, cutting them into individual cards,*

and challenging your ability to correctly guess the symbol on each card while it is face down or hidden. Figure 6.1 continues on page 74.

© Infobase Publishing

Figure 6.1 *Continued from page 73.*

his neighbors, he was fascinated with the idea of survival after death. Rhine intended to enter the ministry until he met Louisa Weckesser. They married in 1919, and he followed her to the University of Chicago, where they both received doctorates in botany with an emphasis on forestry.

Rhine and his wife soon tired of the trees and began pursuing their interest in psychic phenomena. In 1924 Rhine joined the American Society for Psychical Research, led at the time by J. Malcolm Bird. Bird was intrigued by the Boston medium Mina Stinson Crandon who channeled "Margery," and the ASPR *Journal* was full of articles about her talents. Eager to experience "Margery" for themselves, the Rhines had a sitting with Crandon in July 1926. Rhine left the séance quite disillusioned, as he had caught Crandon cheating several times, and he resigned his ASPR membership.

In 1927 Rhine accepted a position at Duke University to work with William McDougall and John F. Thomas in the new Parapsychology Laboratory. He began developing experiments and methodology for scientific study of psychic phenomena and ability, especially PK and ESP, a term he coined. Although his data strongly suggested the existence of psi, Rhine did not publish his findings until 1934. Such conclusions were controversial but lent the new field of parapsychology legitimacy. Rhine believed that the limits of ESP and its probability as the cause for psychokinetic activity had to be established before any real examination of survival after death could be considered, since he doubted that messages from beyond were more than perception by the medium.[126]

Rhine noticed, too, what is called the *experimenter effect.* This means that the person conducting the psi tests consciously or unconsciously influences the results either by preference for a set of answers, animosity toward a particular outcome, or body language that the test subject can sense and which affects his or her responses. Even if the experimenter appears disinterested in the answers, he or she can send thoughts telepathically to the test subject.[127]

Hence the repetitive forced-card tests and experiments with PK. Rhine would turn over cards in another room and have the psychic try and determine which symbol was on the card—a star, circle, square, cross, or parallel wavy lines. There are five of each of the symbols in the 25-card deck. Rhine also used the cards to test clairvoyance by asking the psychic to call down the symbols in order in the deck before any cards were removed or looked at, an experiment called "down through" or "DT" for short.[128] The tests were tedious; psychic Eileen Garrett once complained that the forced-card tests could rapidly reduce a sensitive person just thrumming with activity into a wood block.[129] And the more bored and disinterested the test subject became, the less psi worked.

Rhine founded the *Journal of Parapsychology* in 1937 and continued to head the laboratory at Duke until his retirement in 1965. At that point Rhine moved the lab, renamed the Foundation for Research on the Nature of Man (FRNM), off campus. It was named the Rhine Research Center in 1995 in his honor.

Louisa Rhine, a psychic researcher in her own right, published the first ESP studies with children in 1937 and was the author in 1943 of the first paper on PK studies involving dice throws.

Her major efforts centered upon the examination of the thousands of unsolicited spontaneous cases of paranormal events that had been sent to the Parapsychology Laboratory. There were so many that she chose to evaluate them at face value, even though she and other researchers knew such accounts were often exaggerated. Rhine claimed she was seeking patterns that would point to other research. The most controversial conclusion was Rhine's assertion that the *percipient* (the one "perceiving" the information), not the *agent* (the one sending the information) was the more important. Critics complained that since Rhine was using unsolicited cases that she did not evaluate for authenticity, she was bound to receive more information from percipients. After all, the case senders had perceived, not caused, the phenomena.

Rhine's assertion that the percipient processed telepathic communications without much participation by an agent cut off a main source of proof of survival after death. If agents (the departed spirits) were not responsible for sending apparitions or messages, were they ever able to be contacted in the first place?

Louisa Rhine worked alongside her husband for 60 years and assumed the directorship of the FRNM after his death.[130]

SOCIETY FOR PSYCHICAL RESEARCH

J. B. Rhine's Parapsychology Laboratory at Duke University may have conducted the first truly scientific research into psychic phenomena, but it was by no means the first institution to investigate the paranormal. Edmund Gurney, Frederic William Henry Myers, and Henry

Sidgwick, all Fellows of Trinity College, Cambridge, founded the Society for Psychical Research (SPR) in London in 1882. All three, but especially Myers, were intrigued by the rise of Spiritualism and formed the society to investigate claims and occurrences of telepathy, mesmerism, hypnotism, clairvoyance, psychic sensitives, apparitions, hauntings, and physical phenomena associated with mediums. Also, they attempted to collect and archive the data and reports associated with these events.

Myers had attended a séance in 1873 conducted by medium C. Williams, who allegedly produced the hairy hand of the popular spirit control John King. Myers first recruited Sidgwick, then gathered together an informal group interested in Spiritualism and the investigation of supernatural phenomena, including Gurney, Arthur Balfour, and Balfour's sister Eleanor. Eleanor Balfour married Henry Sidgwick in 1876, and the fledgling paranormal investigators called themselves "the Sidgwick group."

Famous members of the SPR included Sir William Crookes, Carl Jung, Sigmund Freud, Mark Twain, Lewis Carroll, J. B. Rhine, and Alfred, Lord Tennyson. By 1910 all of the original male participants were dead, but they reportedly validated survival by contact through mediums. These early researchers believed in the possibility of psychic communication and only sought to expose trickery in order to bolster those psychics who really possessed the power.[131]

The SPR remains active with a current membership of about 5,500 and annual revenues of £5.2 million (about $10.4 million). The society has expanded its interests and investigations to include out-of-body experiences, remote viewing, psychokinesis, poltergeists, levitation, teleportation, dreams, trances, automatic writing, reincarnation, the social and psychological ramifications of paranormal phenomena across different cultures, and the development of new theories and scientific methods of research. Additionally, the SPR has amassed an extensive library and archive of the history of psychic occurrences.[132]

THE AMERICAN SOCIETY FOR PSYCHICAL RESEARCH

Following the lead of their British counterparts, the American Society for Psychical Research (ASPR) was organized in Boston in 1885 under the presidency of astronomer Simon Newcomb. The group was dedicated to the investigation of paranormal phenomena. Originally a separate society, financial difficulties forced the ASPR to reorganize as a chapter of the SPR in 1890 under the leadership of Richard Hodgson until his death in 1905. In 1906, the ASPR again became independent, led by James H. Hyslop, and moved to New York.[133]

After Hyslop's death in 1920 the society began favoring its Spiritualist faction and mediumship rather than more impartial investigation of psychic activity. Those opposed to the emphasis on séances split off from the ASPR in 1923 and formed the Boston Society for Psychical Research. The two groups did not reunite until 1941.

At that point psychologists were following the lead of researchers such as J. B. Rhine. Gardner Murphy, who headed the new ASPR from 1962-1971, returned the society to an investigative organization. Murphy was joined by Karlis Osis, a psychic researcher of deathbed apparitions. Their efforts led to a $1 million bequest from the estate of Chester E. Carlson, inventor of the Xerox photocopying process.[134]

Probably the most famous member of the ASPR was philosopher William James. James, a Harvard professor and brother of author Henry James, tried to remain out of the "ghosthunting" fray. It was his very position, however, that lent credibility to the society's efforts. James tested trance medium Leonora Piper and found her to be genuine and astoundingly accurate.

Despite his reluctance to investigate the paranormal, James continued, hoping to find another gifted psychic like Leonora Piper. So did many other eminent scientists and philosophers of the day. Why did they risk ridicule and disappointment? In *Ghost Hunters*, author Deborah Blum says that in an age of rapid, impersonal, technological

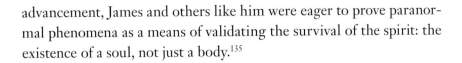

advancement, James and others like him were eager to prove paranormal phenomena as a means of validating the survival of the spirit: the existence of a soul, not just a body.[135]

INSTITUT MÈTAPSYCHIQUE INTERNATIONALE

Founded in Paris with the generous backing of French Spiritualist Jean Meyer, the Institut Mètapsychique Internationale (IMI) opened its doors in 1918 under the directorship of Gustave Geley. The IMI studied the physical mediumship of Marthe Beraud and her control Eva C., and Willi and Rudi Schneider, brothers and psychics from Austria.

The Institut never recovered from the upheaval of World War II. Although still in operation, it is quite small and only opens by appointment.[136]

WILLLIAM GEORGE ROLL (1926–)

A long-time researcher of proof of survival after death, Roll is best known as an expert on psychokinesis and poltergeist activity. During an investigation of unusual disturbances at a home in Seaford, Long Island, in 1958, he and fellow researcher Joseph Gaither Pratt (commonly called J. G. Pratt) found that the mysterious events taking place there—objects flying about the room and crashing against the walls, bottles of holy water exploding—were the result of concentrated energy impulses from a 12-year-old boy. Roll and Pratt coined the term *recurrent spontaneous psychokinesis (RSPK)* to explain the phenomena, and it has become synonymous with poltergeist activity.[137]

Roll was born in Bremen, Germany. During his childhood, Roll had several out-of-body experiences (OBE), and these strange events led to his career in parapsychology. In 1957, J. B. Rhine invited Roll to join him at Duke in the Parapsychology Laboratory, where he worked for two years. In 1959, a conference at Duke on "Incorporeal

Personal Agency" led to the establishment of the Psychical Research Foundation (PRF), also at Duke, and Roll became its director. The PRF moved to Durham, North Carolina, in 1962 until Roll moved the institute to the State University of Western Georgia (formerly West Georgia College), Carrollton, in 1987.

Roll received his doctorate in psychology from the University of Lund, Sweden, in 1989 and became a professor there in 1990. He continues research into the survival of the spirit but has become more skeptical, believing that after death memory impressions join a huge "psi field" accessible to living persons. Roll still maintains that poltergeists are manifestations of RSPK[138] (see "The Tragedy of Tina Resch" on page 25). He has also worked closely with psychic detective Noreen Renier.

LOYD AUERBACH (c. 1955–)

Auerbach, who grew up fascinated with science fiction and tales of the unexplained on such television shows as *The Twilight Zone*, is director of the Office of Paranormal Investigations in Pleasant Hill, California. He also served as a consulting editor for *FATE* magazine until 2004 and as president of the Psychic Entertainers Association until 2005. He is a magician, an author, and a professor of parapsychology. And while Auerbach doesn't own a proton pack, he is a ghostbuster.[139]

By the early 1980s parapsychology was becoming respectable, and Auerbach received a Masters degree from JFK University in Orinda, California, in 1981. He recently launched a parapsychological certification program in conjunction with HCH Institute (formerly The Hypnosis Clearing House) in Lafayette, California.[140]

Auerbach believes in the existence of psi, but he says he can smell trickery a mile away. He has investigated claims of the paranormal in many locations and produced a documentary on the ghosts of the USS *Hornet*.[141] His first book, *ESP, Hauntings and Poltergeists* (1986), has been designated the definitive text on ghosts. (He wanted to name the book *I Ain't Afraid of No Ghost*, but by 1986 that phrase was permanently associated with the *Ghostbusters* movie.)[142]

Auerbach appears often in the media. In addition to its investigative services, his Office of Paranormal Investigations serves as a resource center for individuals, companies, and members of the media seeking credible information on psychic events.

DR. GARY SCHWARTZ (c. 1945–)

Dr. Gary Schwartz directs The Veritas Research Program in the Laboratory for Advances in Consciousness and Health, formerly called the Human Energy Systems Laboratory, in the Department of Psychology at the University of Arizona, Tucson.[143]   He has tested scores of mediums, including John Edward and Allison DuBois, to either verify or deny their professed abilities and feels that the success rates achieved in his experiments prove survival of consciousness. Ray Hyman, skeptic and sometime palm reader, refutes Schwartz's conclusions, noting that once an observer accepts the supposed accuracy of a medium's reading, it is nearly impossible to change that belief.[144]

Schwartz noodled with his ideas of survival for years but did not begin actual research on the subject until the 1990s. His early work at Yale centered on psychophysiology, or the mind-body connection. Schwartz moved to the University of Arizona in 1988, where he felt less pressure to conform to traditional lines of thought. One of Schwartz's theories is that whenever two things share energy and/or information, they form what he calls a "feedback system." Over time these accumulated exchanges become part of the universe's collective memory and could ultimately prove the survival of consciousness after death.[145]

Tests of John Edward and later Allison DuBois often required the psychics to deduce as much information as possible from an unknown, unseen, silent sitter in another room. Both psychics but especially

DuBois found this difficult; she couldn't establish empathy with the sitter or receive validation of her impressions. The psychics had a 77 percent "hit rate" even when they knew nothing about the sitter and 85 percent when they could interact.[146] Nevertheless, these outstanding results did not convince the skeptics that psi exists.

Psychic, Schmychic:
It's All a Trick

The famous illusionist and escape artist Harry Houdini died on Halloween, October 31, 1926. One of the greatest magicians ever, Houdini accomplished amazing feats, especially seemingly impossible escapes, that have not been repeated by any other performer. How he did them remains a mystery.

Houdini lived in magical times. The enormous technological advancements of the late nineteenth and early twentieth centuries inspired some and terrified others. Some feared science would prove there was no hereafter. Seeking proof of an afterlife, many turned to Spiritualism, which offered affirmation and communication with those who had passed. But too many Spiritualist practitioners were charlatans, employing clever tricks to fleece the public. Houdini spent a good part of his life exposing these con artists.

Nevertheless, after the death of his mother, Cecilia Weiss, Houdini desperately tried to contact her. In June 1922, Houdini and his wife, Bess, were traveling with Sir Arthur Conan Doyle and his wife, Jean. Lady Doyle offered her services as an inspired writer (meaning she practiced automatic writing) to see if she could get through. Lady Doyle soon covered an entire sheet of paper with messages to her "darling boy." Sir Arthur, who did not believe Houdini could perform his death-defying escapes *without* spirit intervention, claimed Houdini was overwhelmed.

In fact, Houdini was not. The first mark Lady Doyle had written was a cross, and Mrs. Weiss was Jewish. Secondly, the Hungarian-born Weiss spoke broken English, and her speech would not have been transcribed so clearly. And most telling, the sitting occurred on June 17, Mrs. Weiss's birthday, yet she made no mention of it. Lady Doyle tried to defend herself, but Houdini remained a skeptic.[147]

Houdini believed, however, that if anyone could escape the veil of death it was he. Right before he died of peritonitis from a ruptured appendix, Houdini worked out a secret phrase with Bess using the mind-reading code they had used in their psychic act. In 1929, Bess agreed to a séance with Arthur Ford, pastor of the First Spiritualist Church of New York. During the sitting, Ford supposedly began channeling Houdini, who recited, "Rosabelle, answer, tell, pray, answer, look, tell, answer, answer, tell." The phrase was part of a song lyric engraved in Bess's wedding band and the secret password. Bess thought Harry had broken through until she learned later that the code phrase had appeared in a 1927 biography of her husband. Bess continued holding séances on Halloween for a few more years but never heard from Harry. Disgusted, Bess said when she died she wouldn't even try to come back. Houdini once said that you can talk to the dead, but they don't answer.[148]

Figure 7.1 *A poster for one of Houdini's performances at a time when the magician and escape artist was debunking fraudulent spiritualists.* (CORBIS)

Like that of William James and the first members of the Society for Psychical Research,

Head Games

Harry Houdini and his wife, Bess, had a great *mentalist* (mind reading) act in the early years of their marriage. They had worked out a code, understandable only to them, by which one would use certain words (and remember, these words had to sound normal in conversation or the audience would have caught on) to tell the other partner information about the volunteer. Then when the partner playing the mind reader revealed something "secret" about the volunteer, the audience gasped in amazement.

Skeptics such as James Randi, *Skeptic* publisher Michael Shermer, and Paul Kurtz contend that mastering these techniques is *all* the psychics have achieved, not the ability to get in touch with the paranormal.

- ○ *Cold Reading.* The method that skeptics assert psychics use most often. By throwing out a barrage of vague terms or by listing a great deal of generic information that could apply to many people, the psychic hopes someone recognizes something and bites.[149] Once the psychic has a "hit," he tries to narrow down his guesses to be more specific, and the questioner is astounded. But once the psychic gets positive feedback from a questioner, the questioner, not the psychic, is actually doing the reading.[150]

- ○ *Warm Reading.* In a warm reading, practiced mentalists rely on well-known psychological principles to gain information, such as the likelihood of wearing a piece of jewelry that belonged to a loved one or keeping a photograph of that person. The psychic asks, perhaps, about a ring or a photo and scores another hit.[151]

- ○ *Hot Reading.* Hot reading utilizes actual information about a questioner obtained ahead of time, either by chance or by cheating. For example, prior to a television appearance, a psychic might pump the producers for information about the audience and then use it later as if he had supernatural knowledge.[152]

Houdini's skepticism was based really on the disappointments he encountered in his search for the proof he so badly wanted.

Most of today's skeptics, however, classify psi phenomena as "pseudoscience" and do not accept the authenticity of its practitioners or the methods of its investigators. Any bad prediction, a "miss," supports the skeptic's position. One could make the argument that sometimes the skeptics respond with their official position before fully investigating the psi event, but still the question remains: Why can't psychics see the really big stuff before it happens?

JAMES RANDI (1928–)

Perhaps the most well-known skeptic and debunker, Randi was born Randall James Hamilton Zwinge in Toronto, Canada. Called "The Amazing Randi," he became a professional magician in 1946 and successfully repeated many of Houdini's illusions. One of Randi's most famous stunts was escaping from a straitjacket while hanging upside down over Niagara Falls. Randi took up Houdini's campaign to expose psychic trickery as well, an effort that has brought him both praise and recrimination since he was 15.[153]

Randi rose to public prominence in 1972 when he attempted to prove that the ability of Israeli psychic Uri Geller to bend spoons and cause clocks and watches to speed up or slow down was a magician's trick, not a PK occurrence.[154] In 1976, Randi helped found the Committee for the Scientific Investigation of Claims of the Paranormal (CSICOP), but he resigned when his feud with Geller caused CSICOP to request that he keep a lower profile. Randi established the James Randi Educational Foundation (JREF) in 1996 and updates its online newsletter, *Swift*, on Fridays. He also writes for *Skeptic* magazine, published by The Skeptics Society. Randi appears frequently on radio and television, sometimes as part of a panel of debunkers vs. a group of psychics.[155]

Figure 7.2 *James Randi, well-known magician and skeptic, has published numerous books on magic, mystery tricks, and hoaxes.* (Jeffery Allan Salter/Corbis)

In September of 2001, Randi claims that Sylvia Browne agreed on television to be tested by the JREF to prove the existence of her psi powers. Both sides would specify before the examination what constituted proof; if Browne succeeded, she would win $1 million. As of the start of 2007, Browne still has not submitted to testing.[156] She suggests on her Web site that Randi donate the money to his favorite charity.[157]

COMMITTEE FOR THE SCIENTIFIC INVESTIGATION OF CLAIMS OF THE PARANORMAL (CSICOP)

The Committee for the Scientific Investigation of Claims of the Paranormal (CSICOP) was founded in 1976 at State University of New York (SUNY) in Buffalo to encourage critical assessment of paranormal claims from a responsible, scientific perspective. The organization maintains a network of investigators, all dedicated to debunking pseudoscience, including the Skeptics Society at Caltech in Pasadena, California, the Tampa Bay (Florida) Skeptics, the North Texas Skeptics based in Carrollton, and the Society for Sensible Exploration outside Seattle. CSICOP also has a large library of research reports and reviews of published material about the paranormal.

In addition to hosting conferences to review members' scientific findings, CSICOP publishes *The Skeptical Inquirer*. The group's founders include Isaac Asimov, Carl Sagan, Martin Gardner, Ray Hyman, and Sidney Hook, as well as James Randi.[158] Paul Kurtz, founding fellow and chairman, is a philosophy professor at SUNY.

Critics complain that CSICOP's members, mostly men, jump to conclusions too quickly and are predisposed to debunking any unusual incident no matter the evidence. And while scientists founded the organization, many of its members are magicians. CSICOP is the world's largest skeptical society.[159]

Psychics John Edward and James Van Praagh have been the focus of several CSICOP investigations. Various skeptics believe the two men might be better *cold readers* (gifted guessers) than psychics. Fans of Edward and Van Praagh disagree.

Skeptics also point to an incident on *Crossing Over With John Edward* in which the replies of an audience member were reportedly misrepresented during the show's taping. The audience member suspected that the production crew was collecting information on audience participants before the taping, but Edward and his staff deny that possibility.[160]

John Edward says that investigator Dr. Gary Schwartz told him that Michael Jordan, arguably the best basketball player ever, only makes 45 percent of his shots on a good day.[161] Why should a psychic be held to a higher standard?

Paul Kurtz, chairman of CSICOP, says that sitters often consult a psychic in times of grief or emotional vulnerability, and an incorrect reading or misguided remark could be distressing for those individuals.[162] On the other hand, if the psychic has provided imperfect information that nevertheless comforts the sitter, should the psychic's mistakes be totally dismissed?

There is no absolute answer to this dilemma, only a matter of acceptance or rejection of the possibility of psi phenomena. In his 1998 interview with Dean Radin about Radin's book *The Conscious Universe*, Jordan Gruber remarked that if a conservative but open-minded scientist were to read Radin's book, that scientist would be so overcome with evidence of psi that a change of mind would occur. Radin replied that he had received great feedback from open-minded yet skeptical people,[163] but the dedicated debunkers remain unconvinced.

THE ACCURACY OF DEREK ACORAH

Parapsychologist and lecturer Dr. Ciaran O'Keeffe joined the cast of the television program *Most Haunted* in April 2004 and soon had questions about Acorah's psychic abilities. Acorah sometimes gave

The Hodgson Report

If a person had embraced Spiritualism in the latter part of the nineteenth century, that individual might also have explored Theosophy, a philosophy claiming that through reincarnation and study of traditional occult mythologies, a person could achieve spiritual oneness with the Supreme Being. One would learn this ancient wisdom from teachers who had reached an exalted level of enlightenment, a group called the Ascended Masters of the Great White Brotherhood.

The Theosophical Society was founded in 1875 by Russian psychic Helena Petrovna Blavatsky, known as HPB (1831–1891), and by Henry Steel Olcott (1832–1907), a former colonel, journalist, and spiritual seeker. Olcott was taken with HPB's apparent familiarity with some of the Ascended Masters, alleged Eastern adepts whom Madame Blavatsky called Morya, Koot Hoomi, and Lal Singh. When Olcott received a letter from another supposed Master, Tuitit Bey, instructing him to study with HPB, he embraced Theosophy and became her disciple for life.[164]

The charismatic Madame Blavatsky could have won converts in any profession, no matter what it might have been. She flouted nineteenth century conventions of respectability, going and doing whatever she pleased. Capitalizing on the popularity of the occult, Madame Blavatsky, who did possess psychic power, claimed she was clairvoyant, clairaudient, clairsentient, had out-of-body experiences, and even that she could levitate.

By 1882, HPB had moved the headquarters of the Society to Adyar, India, near Madras, supposedly to be nearer to the Ascended Masters, most of whom apparently came from the area. She had a shrine room built within the main building with sliding panels to ease communication, and settled her former colleague Emma Cutting, now Coulomb, and her husband in Adyar to manage the household.[165]

The Coulombs saw their new position as an ideal platform for blackmail. While HPB traveled in Europe with Olcott, the Coulombs confided to the London *Times* that Emma had letters from HPB giving her, Emma, instructions to fake the mysterious appearances and letters from the

Ascended Masters. Emma claimed she had been told to place the forgeries in the cabinet, which was accessed from HPB's bedroom.[166]

Such revelations rocked the Theosophical world and caught the attention of the Society for Psychical Research. The SPR sent Richard Hodgson to Madras to investigate, but the cabinet had been chopped up and burned. The loyal Olcott said it had been destroyed to protect Madame Blavatsky's reputation.

When Hodgson visited the Coulombs' apartment in Madras, he received a mysterious letter. Emma Coulomb demonstrated how the letter dropped from the ceiling by attachment to a nearly invisible thread on a hook.

Figure 7.3   *Russian psychic Helena Petrovna Blavatsky founded The Theosophical Society.* (Bettman/ CORBIS)

Hodgson's meticulous 350-page report supported Emma Coulomb's claim that HPB had written the letters from the Ascended Masters. Blavatsky was branded an imposter.[167]

For her part, Madame Blavatsky wrote that Hodgson would be shown to be ignorant of the very ideas he had been sent to investigate. And that may be true. More than a century later, Vernon G. Harrison, a British physicist, member of the SPR, and researcher who worked on disputed documents, examined the Hodgson Report and found it flawed and uncorroborated. He took issue with the report's conclusions and lack of carefully tested evidence. Harrison therefore said there was no proof that Madame Blavatsky wrote the letters from the Masters.[168]

Of course, there was no proof she didn't, either.

out conflicting information about a supernatural event, and on two occasions described details about alleged spirits that were in truth concocted by O'Keeffe. O'Keeffe published his "exposé" in the *Daily Mirror*, creating a minor scandal and initially shocking some fans of the show.[169] The incident blew over when *Most Haunted* was deemed entertainment, not news, and Acorah was not held accountable.

Becoming a Psychic

Now that psi has been defined, some of the research analyzed, famous psychics introduced, and testing groups scrutinized, it is time to lay out the procedures for developing psychic ability. One might be quite good at predicting what song will play next on the radio, but that skill alone doesn't guarantee psi proficiency. If a budding psychic doesn't have an ancestor who can pass on psi ability, study and practice is the best method for sharpening one's skills and subtle perceptions. (Most people would prefer not suffering a head injury just to talk to dear, departed Aunt Martha.) There are a number of techniques and practice exercises one can use to facilitate tuning into the psychic frequency.

IDENTIFYING YOUNG PSYCHICS

Allison DuBois, who tried to ignore her paranormal gifts when she was a child, encourages young people to pursue their gift and urges the parents of would-be psychics to recognize and validate their child's powers through love and support. She suggests asking the following questions:[170]

- Do you fluster easily in certain situations or complain of being crowded in a relatively empty room?

- Do you find being in a room with too many people overwhelming?

- Have you ever seen apparitions or figures that others can't see, and could you give detailed descriptions of what you saw?

- Have you foreseen events that later came to pass or identified locations of events or hidden items?[171]

These questions can apply to any young, would-be psychic, like a younger brother or sister or maybe the kid next door who seems to know things others don't notice. To sharpen a younger child's skills, try to devise games and fun tests. For adolescents, practice on friends and family and try not to take it too seriously if the messages or impressions are a bit twisted at first; skill will come.[172] Meditation or visualization of a white light expanding outward from the heart throughout the body and beyond helps calm anxiety.[173]

DuBois offers these suggestions as a way of recognizing young psychics who already possess the gift, not creating them, and Chris Dufresne, Sylvia Browne's son, agrees. He counsels beginners to practice good health habits, not take drugs, take time to meditate or relax to release negative energy, and practice skills like forced-card reading, automatic writing, guessing the contents of envelopes, or trying to "see" hidden messages.[174]

Although he had psychic experiences early in life, James Van Praagh writes that he sharpened his powers through exercises such as closing his eyes and trying to sense feelings—vibrations—from an unknown object he was trying to identify. He practiced describing an unknown person who was standing a few feet behind him, unseen, or he would try to "see" what colors his coworkers might be wearing to work that day before they arrived. He read every book he could find on psychic behavior, too.[175]

TRYING ON PSI FOR SIZE

Before making a career change, it is always smart to check out the type of work one might be expected to do and the environment of that work. Is it challenging? Is it people oriented or rather solitary? What's the average salary?

Unless one knows a practicing psychic personally, a good way to watch a reading in action is at a psychic fair. In some communities, one is held someplace in town almost every weekend. Participants might include the readers, pet psychics, those who sell and read crystals, various craftspeople who create jewelry or work with stones, and holistic healers or other alternative therapy specialists.

The cost of a reading at a fair should be more affordable than at a private session, since the allotted time is shorter. *Never* give a reader additional money to facilitate a clearer message or to psychically improve the situation, and don't give out credit card numbers. Requests like that might be a scam.

Don't be too concerned if the reading doesn't quite sound pertinent. The psychic is trying to receive information, but some readings are inconclusive or vague. And don't assume that all psychics would give the same interpretation to identical Tarot card spreads or from impressions received from other divination tools. Most important, if it feels like something is fishy with the psychic or the location of the reading, leave.

CREATING PSYCHICS

Author Nathaniel Friedland in his book *Be Psychic Now!* confidently asserts that each of us has the potential to exhibit psi. Friedland started as a telephone psychic. He advocates meditation to slow the breath rate and to focus attention. Clear the mind and maintain a state of relaxed awareness, and eventually one's heightened senses will begin to respond with paranormal impressions.[176]

In *Psychic Development for Beginners*, author William W. Hewitt claims he was just an ordinary person until he developed his psychic sensitivities through a series of easy mental exercises.[177] Hewitt begins with visualization then proceeds to sensing an unknown object's color.

Relaxation techniques are vital to allowing the body to be open to new sensations and energies, allowing the mind to pick up spiritual messages about the future.[178] Of course, visualization and deep breathing enhance any effort to relax and attune to the surroundings.

The Art of Psi

Paul Huson suggests what he calls *picture-drawing tests*, traditionally reliable indicators of psychic ability. Upton Sinclair, the early twentieth century author and social reformer, conducted picture tests with his wife for more than three years. Albert Einstein was so impressed by the Sinclairs' results that he wrote the introduction to *Mental Radio* (1930), Sinclair's book about the couple's experiments. As always, Einstein was years ahead of his time; the parapsychological research he so heartily endorsed didn't gain much credibility until the 1970s.[179]

Try and find a partner for the test who is open to the idea of ESP and who could be described as warm, sociable, talkative, easygoing, happy—in other words, a person comfortable with new possibilities. Working with a partner who can be described this way illustrates the *sheep-goat effect:* test results with friendly, optimistic people (sheep) have a much higher chance of producing psi than with people who are grumpy, angry, or disinterested in the process (goats).[180]

One partner should be in one room, if possible, drawing whatever comes to mind (don't worry about artistic talent), while the other person is in a different room, waiting for the first person to finish. When the picture is complete, the partner can begin drawing. The goal is for the second artist to pick up impressions of what the first artist drew and repeat the main points of the picture. Try this exercise several times, for it may take a while for the commonalities in the drawings to appear.

Huson comments that sometimes the similarities in the drawings are truly spectacular.[181] He likens the connection between our thoughts and the pictures to the act of dreaming, since we weave our conscious thoughts into subconscious pictures in our sleep.[182]

Huson also recommends forced-card tests, in which one person turns over a card and the other person tries to guess what that card is. A standard Zener deck has five cards each of five symbols—the ever-popular circle, star, double wavy lines, square, and cross—but any five symbols on pieces of paper will do.[183]

Hands-on Psi

Finally, there are the exercises in psychometry. In her book *The Complete Guide to Psychic Development*, Cassandra Eason suggests beginners start by trying to read something that has a long history within a family, like a teacup from Great-Grandmother's china. Don't worry too much about whether the impressions received make sense to the item's owner. They may later. If the mental pictures are hazy, try imagining the day Great-Grandmother received the china or some other connection. Above all, *practice*.[184]

Realizing the presence of psi may be cool, but there are some definite pitfalls to avoid. Many psychics are afraid of the unknown and of losing control or their grasp of reality. They often suffer from depression or feel isolated and take on the pain or unhappiness of others in sympathy with them.[185] Working as a psychic is a big responsibility. It's one thing to predict songs on the radio but quite another to give people information about their loved ones that could be wrong or even hurtful. Be confident yet respectful. Look into the future with courage. After all, reading the future is the most important thing that a psychic does.[186]

Paul Huson writes that, "There is ample evidence that psychic ability not only lies in each and every one of us but may well constitute the very foundation of our everyday lives, although we are not aware of it." He goes on to paraphrase William James, who said the problem was not so much how to perform psychically but how to tap into our abilities and make them a reality.[187]

Having the power to access worlds beyond the reach of most people is truly a gift and should be cherished, fostered, and developed to its full potential. The comfort and understanding that a sensitive psychic can provide cannot be measured, only accepted with gratitude.

Go for it.

9

Talking—and Listening —to the Animals

Jaytee was a mixed-breed terrier that lived in northwest England with his owner, Pam Smart, in a ground-level apartment next door to her parents. She adopted him from the Manchester Dogs' Home in 1989, and they were very good friends. For a long time Pam's parents noticed that Jaytee would go to the window and look for Pam to come home. In the beginning Pam had regular hours, so that Jaytee's behavior was believed to be routine. But after Pam was laid off and came and went with no pattern, Jaytee still anticipated her return at least 85 percent of the time.

Pam's parents began keeping a log of Jaytee's behavior and found that the dog usually jumped up in front of the window when Pam decided to go home, not when she was close to arrival. Working with animal researcher Rupert Sheldrake, the family videotaped Jaytee, leaving the recorder running. The tapes consistently showed Jaytee anticipating Pam's return home. They tested Jaytee several ways, changing Pam's time of departure, the time she thought about leaving, her mode of transportation, and the distance between her transportation drop-off point and her apartment. Still Jaytee knew. Is it telepathy between dog and human or something else?[188]

PSYCHIC ANIMALS

Sheldrake believes such communication is indeed telepathy. In his studies of domesticated animals—dogs, cats, horses, sheep, pigs, small rodents, hens, ducks, geese, cattle, and goats—he has accumulated hundreds of anecdotes about how these animals not only anticipate their masters' returns but exhibit extraordinary powers of homing, directional sense, healing, and detection and/or warning of danger and disease.[189] To possess such powers, the animals must come from a species that cares for its young. A strong pet/owner relationship, a social bond, is also necessary. Reptiles, amphibians, and fish live independently and don't interact with their young, and

Figure 9.1 *A woman and her guide dog walk down the aisle of a supermarket. Some animal researchers report telepathic connections between animal owners and their pets.* (Steven King/AP)

Sheldrake did not find any telepathic bond between humans and these species.[190]

As a long-time animal researcher and pet owner, Sheldrake takes issue with scientists who smugly dismiss the anecdotal evidence supplied by pet owners, trainers, zoo personnel, and other animal workers. Such scientists want hard numbers, experiments that can be repeated in a laboratory, and results that can be tested technologically. Sheldrake notes, however, that *anecdotal* means "not published": medical hypotheses have become breakthroughs when the researcher's anecdotal observations appeared in professional journals.

Sheldrake is convinced that many animals possess psi, commonly called **animal psi** or **anpsi**. Their abilities fall into one of three categories: telepathy, directional sense, and precognition.[191] Telepathy covers the animals who know in advance when their owners are coming home; the ones who know when their owners are on the other end of a phone call; the dogs, in particular, who act strangely or frantically at precisely the same time some tragedy befalls their owners, even over long distances; and the animals, often cats, who sense pain or illness and stay close, offering warmth and comfort. Sheldrake received accounts of pets realizing their owners were having emotional breakdowns, even saving them from suicide.

Animals are great healers. Some hospitals and nursing homes allow pets to stay with their owners, while others have added animal visits to the recovery routine, resulting in happier patients and lower rates of blood pressure and pulse. Therapeutic horse programs provide support and encouragement for both children and adults suffering physical and mental disabilities.[192] Many facilities for troubled kids now include animal care as a means of redirecting anger and resentment into love and responsibility.

Animals' directional sense includes their unerring ability to *home*: to know how to return home even from far away. Scientists have always been interested in animal instinct, but Sheldrake sees homing as a more highly defined skill. He has documented animals who have returned home by traveling over great, unfamiliar terrain, like the two dogs and a cat in the 1961 novel *The Incredible Journey*, which was twice made into a movie by Disney, once in 1963 as *The Incredible Journey* and in 1993 as *Homeward Bound: The Incredible Journey*. Perhaps the most amazing directional feat is that of animals who seek and find their owners. They're not headed to a place they know but are searching unknown territory for the *person* they know and love.

Precognition in animals can be seen most clearly in two ways: pets who know in advance when their owners are going to have an epileptic seizure and warn them accordingly and animals' strange behavior before earthquakes.

People with epilepsy can suffer a seizure at any time, often without warning. Many of the seizures are small, even unnoticed, but a major episode can cause rigidity, falls, labored breathing, a swallowed tongue, and convulsions.[193] In his research, Sheldrake collected accounts of how the pets—principally dogs—of epileptics not only warned their owners but often nudged them to a chair or bed to protect them from falling. Some of these amazing animals could even sense an oncoming seizure from another room. A few knew what programmed button to push on the telephone to bark for help! According to their owners, none of these pets had been trained; they just knew what to do.

Epilepsy is not the only disease that animals can sense. There are dogs that recognize when a diabetic's blood sugar is low, risking a seizure or even death. And some dogs may even be capable of sensing cancer. In 1989, two British dermatologists removed a malignant melanoma from a patient who commented that her dog kept bothering what she thought was a mole.[194]

Michael McCulloch and Michael Broffman, scientists at the Pine Street Foundation, an alternative medicine center in San Anselmo, California, used ordinary dogs to sniff breath samples of patients with and without breast and lung cancer. The dogs' success rate was an astounding 88 percent for breast cancer and a whopping 99 percent for lung. In another study, canines identified bladder cancer victims by smelling their urine; the dogs scored hits about 41 percent of the time.[195]

Despite such impressive results, dogs have not joined the oncology staff. Dr. Donald Berry, head of biostatistics at M.D. Anderson Cancer Center in Houston, said he would like to believe these findings but needed further proof.[196]

Many people have noticed animals exhibiting unusual or outright weird behavior a day or so before an earthquake occurs. Birds congregate or fly in crazy patterns. Cattle become anxious. Dogs and cats hide. And rats flee the area.[197] Unfortunately, according to Sheldrake, scientists who study earthquakes have concentrated on technological and geological clues—which so far have not foretold a quake—instead of observing the animals' behavior patterns.[198]

ANIMAL PSYCHICS

There are people out there who do observe animal patterns of activity and response, understand the creatures' natural tendencies, and have established animal psychology practices to help pets and their owners overcome earlier mistakes or abuses. Some behaviorists claim that they can communicate with the animals psychically to learn the real story of how they have been treated and what they think of their owners.

One man took his dog to a psychic to determine why the dog nipped aggressively. First, the dog supposedly explained the motivation for his behavior—he had been harassed by children in his first home—then complained that his new owner was too uptight about keeping the house clean and tidy.

In 2002, a cable television show entitled *The Pet Psychic* made psychic and former model Sonya Fitzpatrick famous. Fitzpatrick said she had communicated with animals from a very early age, especially after she suffered a major hearing loss. She empathized so completely with her terrier, Judy, that she could feel the dog's pains. The untimely death of three geese she was raising caused Fitzpatrick to deny her

Plants Are Psychic, Too

Some people just seem to have a green thumb. They can grow anything. When asked what the secret is to growing such vigorous plants, the answer might be, "I talk to them." And although talking to plants might seem like talking to furniture, studies have indicated that plants are as sensitive as people and actually respond to speech.[199]

While conducting a training session on polygraph equipment for a police department, Cleve Backster decided to attach the electrodes to a dracaena leaf to see how the plant might react to both tender attention and fear of pain. He thought briefly about burning the leaf to get a better reading, but that wasn't necessary; the printout on the polygraph spiked up dramatically, which Backster interpreted as fear of fire by the plant. Backster claims that further testing indicated that plants love humans and trust them, even accepting salt water (usually bad for plants) and flourishing on it if administered by a person the plant likes! Plants also express alarm and distress if their humans are ill or wounded; Backster's plant indicated concern over the blood from a cut finger.[200]

Probably the most amazing results with plant psi, however, suggest that plants respond to prayer. In experiments conducted in the 1970s by Robert N. Miller, a scientist at Lockheed Aircraft Corporation, psychic healer Olga Worrall stood at least 60 feet away from a bed of rye grass seeds and visualized that the seeds were filled with light and energy. The rye seeds' rates of growth and germination subsequently jumped 840 percent.

In other tests of the growth rate of a single blade of Worrall's rye grass, Miller found that the grass's growth per hour sped up 830 percent, from .00625 inches to .0525 inches, when Worrall and her husband Ambrose prayed for the successful maturation of the grass. Astoundingly, in that experiment, the Worralls were more than 600 miles away.[201]

psychic skills. Fitzpatrick pursued a career in fashion modeling, then moved from her native England to Houston, Texas, in 1991 to become an etiquette consultant. A spiritual experience in 1994 renewed her psychic abilities.[202] Fitzpatrick claims she can channel the spirits of pets to provide messages to their former owners.

Other animal psychics, also known as communicators, have been popular in the media and with the public. Toni Trimble, a Texan who specializes in communications with horses, might be called a "horse whisperer": someone who seems to have a particular bond with that animal. Such a person was the hero of Nicholas Evans' 1995 bestseller, *The Horse Whisperer*, which was made into a movie with Robert Redford in 1998. "Whisperer" has become synonymous with anyone who communicates in a seemingly psychic manner, even with the spirits.

Cesar Millan, the "dog whisperer," also has a show on cable television. His canine behavioral techniques depend on establishing the owners as "pack leaders," since dogs are pack animals. Millan, who owns approximately 50 dogs of different breeds who live together peacefully, stresses "rules, boundaries and limitations" through "exercise, discipline and affection."[203] Mark Derr, a dog trainer and behaviorist from Miami, takes issue with the importance of pack leadership and Millan's emphasis on strenuous exercise. Derr also says that Millan does not give enough affection and positive feedback.[204]

It doesn't matter whether an animal might be considered psychic or a human might have paranormal connections to animals. It is the unconditional love between people and animals that enables such deep understanding. In Vietnamese culture, dogs are just one level below humans in the cycle of reincarnation. Rupert Sheldrake adds that human nature is bound up with that of animals. He believes that people who live without animals lose a portion of their heritage and are diminished[205] as humans, existing with less capacity for love and care.

Timeline

2.5 million years ago   Early evidence of man in Africa

10,000 years ago   "Dragon bones" used for divination in early Chinese settlements along Yellow River

3500-3200 BCE   Stone circles appear

3100   Egyptians begin astrological charting

1193   Fall of Troy; Cassandra's enslavement

1000   Chinese use *I Ching*

700s   Delphi becomes temple for Apollo

680-627   Golden period for Hebrew prophets

587–556   Hebrew exile in Babylonia

213   Emperor Chin orders burning of Confucius' books

5-1   Evidence of Mesopotamian prophecies

150–150 AD   Prophesying flourishes in early Church

1300s   First appearance of playing cards

1392   First appearance of Tarot cards

1400   Palmistry forbidden by the Church

1400s   Tarot cards designed for Visconti-Sforza families

1540s   Nostradamus begins prophesying and writing his revelations in quatrains

1700s   Merger of Tarot cards with regular playing cards to form "Marseilles" deck

1743   Emanuel Swedenborg begins experiencing trances, visions of Heaven

1848   Spiritualism born at Fox home, Hydesville, NY

1850s–1880s   Golden age of Spiritualism

1850s   Planchettes popular in séances

1875   Theosophical Society founded by Madame Helena Petrovna Blavatsky and Colonel Henry Steel Olcott

1882   Founding of Society for Psychical Research

1885   Founding of American Society for Psychical Research

1880s   Leonora Piper convinces William James of the possibility of psychic power

1892   Elijah J. Bond sells patent for Ouija board to William Fuld

1901   Edgar Cayce begins giving readings and psychic healings

1910   Arthur Edward Waite and Pamela Colman Smith introduce Rider-Waite Tarot deck

1918   Institut Mètapsychique Internationale opens

1923   Boston Society for Psychical Research splits off from ASPR

1925   Research on super-psi conducted in London

1926   Harry Houdini dies from peritonitis on Halloween

1927   J.B. Rhine joins Parapsychology Laboratory at Duke University

1934   Rhine begins psychokinesis testing on gambler who claimed he could affect dice rolls

1937   Louisa Rhine tests ESP of children

1943   Louisa Rhine presents first paper on PK tests with dice rolls

1946   James Randi begins career as magician

1948   Louisa Rhine begins examination of spontaneous paranormal events

1956   Jeane Dixon predicts election and assassination of John F. Kennedy

1958   William G. Roll and J. G. Pratt coin term *recurrent spontaneous psychokinesis* during investigation in Seaford, L.I.

1959   Roll establishes Psychical Research Foundation at Duke University

1960   Case of Sauchie Poltergeist

1960s   Helmut Schmidt conducts micro-PK tests using coin-flipper machines

1966   Parker Brothers buys rights to Ouija board

1969   Stanley Krippner, Montague Ullmann and Charles Honorton conduct experiments on dreams

1970s   Ingo Swann changes resting temperature of an object in retro-PK tests; Robert Miller tests effectiveness of prayer on growth of rye grass seeds with Olga Worrall

1972   James Randi allegedly proves spoon-bending by Uri Geller is a trick; Harold Puthoff and Russell Targ begin remote viewing studies at SRI International

1973   Honorton and S. Harper conduct Ganzfield tests at Maimonides Hospital

1974   Sylvia Browne founds Nirvana Foundation for Psychical Research

1976   Committee for the Scientific Investigation of Claims of the Paranormal (CSICOP) founded at SUNY, Buffalo

1980   Stephan A. Schwartz participates in remote viewing project to find ancient parts of city of Alexandria, Egypt

1982   Targ and Keith Harary study remote viewing for experiment on silver speculation

1984   Tina Resch becomes victim of psychokinesis

1986   Publication of *ESP, Hauntings and Poltergeists* by Loyd Auerbach

1988   Gary Schwartz moves to the University of Arizona and later founds the Veritas Program there

1990s   Rupert Sheldrake tests terrier Jaytee

1997   James Spottiswoode notices that psi is more active at 13:30 LST

2000   *Crossing Over with John Edward* premieres

2000–2001   Mick O'Neill begins psi experiments with winning numbers in the British National Lottery

2001   Nostradamus credited with predicting terrorist attack in New York on September 11; James Randi establishes $1 million prize to any psychic that can prove psi abilities

2004   British physicians find dogs can identify bladder cancer patients by smells in urine

2006   Doctors in California announce that dogs can identify breast and lung cancers by smell

Glossary

ANIMAL PSI OR ANPSI The psychic ability of animals, encompassing telepathy, homing and precognition

APPLIED PSI Acknowledgement of psi's existence with more emphasis on how it can be used

CLAIRAUDIENCE French for "clear-hearing"; the ability to psychically hear spirits from beyond or disembodied voices

CLAIRSENTIENCE French for "clear-knowing"; the ability to understand psychically without any apparent involvement by the senses

CLAIRVOYANCE French for "clear-seeing"; second sight; knowing things without benefit of the five senses

DIVINATION General term for any method used to foretell the future

DOWSING An ancient skill used to find water, oil, or other treasure by holding a Y-shaped branch downward and walking until the branch begins to shake, indicating the location of the object sought

EXTRASENSORY PERCEPTION (ESP) The ability to perceive information from some source beyond the limits of the five senses; includes telepathy, clairvoyance and precognition

GANZFIELD German for "entire space"; usually a large field of white, like a blank wall, used to promote development of psi abilities; staring at the field may clear the mind, allowing greater telepathic sensitivity

LEVITATION The ability to overcome gravity and rise and float above the floor or other surface

MEDIUM A psychic individual who can supposedly communicate with the spirits of those who have passed; all mediums are psychic, but not all psychics are mediums

MENTALIST   A performer with a mind-reading act

PARANORMAL   Above or beyond the normal

PARAPSYCHOLOGY   The study of unexplained behaviors generally judged to be above or beyond the expected norm

PHENOMENON (A)   A mysterious or unexplained event or manifestation

POLTERGEIST   German for "noisy ghost"; usually associated with psychokinetic events connected to the intense energy surrounding adolescents

PRECOGNITION   Having foreknowledge

PSI   A more general term for ESP and PK that signifies paranormal abilities but without the requirement of perception or action; has come to refer to any unexplained manifestation

PSYCHIC   *n.* A person who claims to have the ability to see into the future and sense things others cannot; *adj.* to possess that ability

PSYCHOKINESIS (PK)   Any change in the composition of an object, its placement, or the creation of phenomena without any physical contact with that object or manifestation

PSYCHOMETRY   The ability to discern information about a person or place simply by holding an object associated with the person or location

QUATRAIN   A four-line verse; the type of poetic structure chosen by Nostradamus for his predictions. A grouping of 100 of the quatrains is a *centurie*

RECURRENT SPONTANEOUS PSYCHOKINESIS (RSPK)   Term coined by William G. Roll and J. G. Pratt to explain the repeated patterns of objects flying about without an apparent force; RSPK is usually attributable to intense adolescent energy or repressed emotion

REMOTE VIEWING   Visualizing places or objects from a distance, either by "seeing" with psychic sight or through an out-of-body experience

SIDEREAL TIME   Time measured not by the movement of the sun and Earth but by the movements of the constellations, particularly

Libra. Wherever Libra is overhead, the local sidereal time (LST)
is 13:30

SUPER-PSI (FORMERLY SUPER-ESP)   Beefed-up psi abilities; the
capacity to perceive or interact with any type of unexplained
phenomena

TELEPATHY   The connection between two or more minds allowing
interaction between them; sending messages or visualizations by
mental concentration

ZODIAC   Greek for "circus of animals," the 12 signs of the heavens
representing the months of the year on an astrological chart

Endnotes

1. IMDB, "Memorable Quotes from *The Bullwinkle Show* (1961)," The Internet Movie Database. http://www.imdb.com/title/tt0054524/quotes.

2. Rosemary Ellen Guiley, *Harper's Encyclopedia of Mystical and Paranormal Experience* (San Francisco: Harper San Francisco, 1991), 470.

3. Paul Huson, *How to Test and Develop Your ESP* (Lanham, Md.: Madison Books, 2001), 22, 25.

4. Edith Hamilton, *Mythology* (Boston: Little, Brown & Co., 1942), 256, 259.

5. Hamilton, *Mythology*, 292, 351, 354–355.

6. Kenneth C. Davis, *Don't Know Much About Mythology* (New York: HarperCollins, 2005), 365.

7. Paul J. Achtemeier, gen. ed., *Harper's Bible Dictionary* (San Francisco: Harper & Row, 1985), 827.

8. Davis, *Don't Know Much About Mythology*, 238.

9. Achtemeier, *Harper's Bible Dictionary*, 827.

10. Guiley, *Harper's Encyclopedia of Mystical and Paranormal Experience*, 427.

11. Achtemeier, *Harper's Bible Dictionary*, 830.

12. Guiley, *Harper's Encyclopedia of Mystical and Paranormal Experience*, 427.

13. Huson, *How to Test and Develop Your ESP*, 22.

14. Guiley, *Harper's Encyclopedia of Mystical and Paranormal Experience*, 482.

15. Jordan S. Gruber, "An Enlightenment Interview with Dean Radin, Ph.D." http://www.enlightenment.com/media/interviews/radin.html (accessed December 5, 2006).

16. Guiley, *Harper's Encyclopedia of Mystical and Paranormal Experience*, 470.

17. Gruber, "An Enlightenment Interview with Dean Radin, Ph.D.," 8.

18. Dan Barry, "For Once, a Psychic Looks Back," *The New York Times*, April 12, 2006.

19. Guiley, *Harper's Encyclopedia of Mystical and Paranormal Experience*, 28–29.

20. Rosemary Ellen Guiley, *The Encyclopedia of Ghosts and Spirits*, 2nd ed. (New York: Facts on File, 2000), 331.

21. Guiley, *The Encyclopedia of Ghosts and Spirits*, 305.

22. Huson, *How to Test and Develop Your ESP*, 25.

23. William G. Roll and Valerie Storey, *Unleashed: Of Poltergeists and Murder, the Curious Story of Tina Resch* (New York: Paraview Pocket Books, 2004), 10.

24. Ibid, 218–224.

25. Huson, *How to Test and Develop Your ESP*, 27.

26. Guiley, *Harper's Encyclopedia of Mystical and Paranormal Experience*, 109–110.

27. Ibid, 487.

28. Ibid, 471.

29. Rosemary Ellen Guiley, "Luck, Psi and Lotteries—Part II," Visionary Living. http://www.visionaryliving.com/articles/luckpsi-II.php.

30. Huson, *How to Test and Develop Your ESP*, 30.

31. "Allison DuBois: *Medium* TV Show Based on Her Life," About Phoenix. http://phoen ix.about.com/od/famous/a/dubois.htm.

32. IMBD, "*Fiddler on the Roof* (1971)", Internet Movie Database. http://www.imdb.com /title/tt0067093/combined#comment.

33. Guiley, *The Encyclopedia of Ghosts and Spirits*, 110–111.

34. Guiley, *The Encyclopedia of Ghosts and Spirits*, 75.

35. Guiley, *Harper's Encyclopedia of Mystical and Paranormal Experience*, 225–226.

36. Ibid, 479–480.

37. Ibid, 480.

38. Ibid, 481.

39. William Braud, "Wellness Implications of Retroactive Influence Exploring an Outrageous Hypothesis," Membersaol.com. http://www.membersaol.com/neonoetics/Bra ud_Retro.html.

40. Guiley, *Harper's Encyclopedia of Mystical and Paranormal Experience*, 481.

41. Ibid, 587–588.

42. Guiley, *The Encyclopedia of Ghosts and Spirits*, 371.

43. Tom Dirks, "*The Exorcist* (1973)," Filmsite. http://www.filmsite.org/exor2.html.

44. Guiley, *Harper's Encyclopedia of Mystical and Paranormal Experience*, 418–419.

45. Rosemary Ellen Guiley, *Encyclopedia of the Strange, Mystical and Unexplained* (New York: Gramercy Books, 2001), 34–36.

46. "Chinese Zodiac," Travel China. http://www.travelchina.com/intro/social_customs/zo diac.

47. Guiley, *Encyclopedia of the Strange, Mystical and Unexplained*, 602–603.

48. Cassandra Eason, *The Complete Guide to Psychic Development* (Berkeley, Calif.: Crossing Press, 2003), 109–113.

49. Rosemary Ellen Guiley, *The Angels Tarot* (San Francisco: HarperSan Francisco, 1995), 2–3.

50. Guiley, *Encyclopedia of the Strange, Mystical and Unexplained*, 602–603.

51. Eason, *The Complete Guide to Psychic Development*, 31.

52. Ibid, 137–138.

53. Ibid, 159.

54. Guiley, *Harper's Encyclopedia of Mystical and Paranormal Experience*, 279–280.

55. Guiley, *Encyclopedia of the Strange, Mystical and Unexplained*, 424–425.

56. Guiley, *Harper's Encyclopedia of Mystical and Paranormal Experience*, 514–515.

57. Eason, *The Complete Guide to Psychic Development*, 40–42, 45.

58. Robert Foster, *Tolkien's World from A to Z: The Complete Guide to Middle-Earth* (New York: Del Ray Books, 1978), 196, 396.

59. Susanna Clarke, *Jonathan Strange and Mr. Norrell* (New York: Bloomsbury Publishing, 2004), 259.

60. "Nostradamus' Biography," Crystalinks. http://www. crystalinks.com/nostradamus.html (accessed August 21, 2006).

61. Tom Harris, "How Nostradamus Works: It's Good to Know," HowStuffWorks. http://science. howstuffworks.com/nostradamus. htm.

62. "9/11/01: Tragedy in the US," Morgana's Observatory. http:// www.dreamscape.com/ morgana/ 91101.htm.

63. Eric Cheatham, "Quatrains of Nostradamus: Interpretation," Crystalinks. http://www.crystalinks. com/quatraininterpretations.html.

64. "Nostradamus: What's a Quatrain?," Active Mind: The Mysterious and Unexplained. http://www.activemind.com/ Mysterious/Topics/Nostradamus/ quatrain.html.

65. Harris, "How Nostradamus Works: It's Good to Know," 2.

66. Guiley, *Harper's Encyclopedia of Mystical and Paranormal Experience*, 590–591.

67. "Emanuel Swedenborg (1688–1772)," Books and Writers. http://www. kirjasto.sci.fi./s weden.htm.

68. "Emanuel Swedenborg," 3.

69. Guiley, *Harper's Encyclopedia of Mystical and Paranormal Experience*, 84.

70. Ibid, 85–86.

71. Michael Kenney, "Stalking the Afterlife," *The Houston Chronicle*, September 10, 2006.

72. Guiley, *The Encyclopedia of Ghosts and Spirits*, 293.

73. Charles Mackay, *Extraordinary Popular Delusions and the Madness of Crowds* (New York: Farrar, Straus and Giroux, 1932), 294.

74. Ibid, 295–296.

75. "Psychic Jeane Dixon Dies," CNN Interactive: SHOWBIZ. http:// www.cnn.com/sho wbiz.9701/26.

76. Ibid.

77. Guiley, *Harper's Encyclopedia of Mystical and Paranormal Experience*, 507.

78. Ibid.

79. Ibid, 508.

80. Joseph McMoneagle, *Memoirs of a Psychic Spy: The Remarkable Life of U.S. Government Remote Viewer 001* (Charlottesville, Va.: Hampton Roads Publishing, 2006), xi.

81. Guiley, *Harper's Encyclopedia of Mystical and Paranormal Experience*, 508.

82. McMoneagle, *Memoirs of a Psychic Spy: The Remarkable Life of U.S. Government Remote Viewer 001*, 132.

83. Guiley, *Harper's Encyclopedia of Mystical and Paranormal Experience*, 508.

84. Stephan A. Schwartz and The Mobius Group, "A Preliminary Survey of the Eastern Harbor, Alexandria, Egypt Including a Comparison of Side Scan Sonar and Remote Viewing," abstract of report delivered to Annual Meeting of the Society for Underwater Archaeology, January 11, 1980, http://www. stephanaschwartz.com/home.htm.

85. Guiley, *Harper's Encyclopedia of Mystical and Paranormal Experience*, 509.

86. Jeffrey A. Trachtenberg, "In Publishing, One Medium Looms Large," *The Wall Street Journal*, March 29, 2006.

87. Emanuel Swedenborg, *De Verbo*, Whitehead, trans., note 3, http://www.heaven lydoctrines.org/Scripts/dtSearch (accessed October 21, 2006).

88. Browne, *Life on the Other Side: A Psychic's Tour of the Afterlife*, 98.

89. Ibid, 104.

90. Ibid, 100.

91. Ibid, 99.

92. Emanuel Swedenborg, *True Christian Religion*, Chadwick, trans., note 794, http://www.heavenly-doctrines.org/Scripts/dtSearch (accessed October 21, 2006).

93. Browne, *Life on the Other Side: A Psychic's Tour of the Afterlife*, 116–119.

94. Emanuel Swedenborg, *True Christian Religion*, Ager, trans., notes 805 and 809, http://www.heaven-lydoctrines.org/Scripts/dtSearch (accessed October 21, 2006).

95. Emanuel Swedenborg, *Heaven and Hell*, Harley, trans., note 384, http://www. heavenlydoctrines. org/Scripts/dtSearch (accessed October 21, 2006).

96. Ibid.

97. Emanuel Swedenborg, *Heaven and Hell*, Ager, trans., note 340, http://www.he avenlydoctrines. org/Scripts/dtSearch (accessed October 21, 2006).

98. Browne, *Life on the Other Side: A Psychic's Tour of the Afterlife*, 101.

99. Ibid, 67.

100. Trachtenberg, "In Publishing, One Medium Looms Large."

101. Sylvia Browne, *Life on the Other Side: A Psychic's Tour of the Afterlife* (New York: Dutton Publishing, 2000), 5–7.

102. Ibid, 13–14.

103. John Edward, *Crossing Over: The Stories Behind the Stories* (San Diego: Jodere Group, 2001), 5–6.

104. "*John Edward/Cross Country* on WE; Season Begins August 25, 2006," The Official John E dward Web Site. http://www.johnedward. net/about_John_Edward.htm.

105. James Van Praagh, *Talking to Heaven: A Medium's Message of Life After Death* (New York: Dutton Publishers, 1999), 7.

106. Ibid, 35.

107. Ibid, 45–47.

108. "James Van Praagh Biography," James Van Praagh Official Web Site. http://www.vanpraagh.com, (accessed January 23, 2006).

109. Allison DuBois, *Don't Kiss Them Good-bye* (New York: A Fireside Book, 2004), 13–16.

110. Ibid, 24–26.

111. Ibid, 17–20, 27–28.

112. Derek Acorah, *The Psychic Adventures of Derek Acorah* (London: HarperElement, 2004), xi–xii.

113. Ibid, 231–235.

114. Ibid, 83–90.

115. Noreen Renier with Naomi Lucks, *A Mind for Murder: The Real-Life Files of a Psychic Investigator* (New York: Berkley Books, 2005), 11–13.

116. Guiley, *Harper's Encyclopedia of Mystical and Paranormal Experience*, 487.

117. Renier, *A Mind For Murder: The Real-Life Files of a Psychic Investigator*, 121–132.

118. "The Laci Peterson Case," CourtTV Online. http://www.courttv.com/talk/chat_transcripts/2004/0722peterson-renier.html (accessed January 30, 2006).

119. *Medium: We See Dead People*, Biography Channel, July 8, 2006.

120. Dr. Dennis McFadden, "Psychic Detectives," The Skeptic's Dictionary. https//websp ace.utexas.edu/cokerwer/www/index.html/detectives.html (accessed October 21, 2006).

121. "Psychic detective," The Skeptic's Dictionary. http://skepdic.com/psychdet.html.

122. DuBois, *Don't Kiss Them Good-bye*, 23.

123. "About Lisa," Lifetime Online. http://www.lifetimetv.com/shows/lisawilliams/bio/ind ex.php (accessed November 7, 2006).

124. IMBD, "*Ghost Busters* (1984)," Internet Movie Database. http://www.imdb.com/titl e/tt0087332.

125. Huson, *How to Test and Develop Your ESP*, 12.

126. Guiley, *The Encyclopedia of Ghosts and Spirits*, 318.

127. Guiley, *Harper's Encyclopedia of Mystical and Paranormal* Experience, 192.

128. Huson, *How to Test and Develop Your ESP*, 177.

129. Huson, *How to Test and Develop Your ESP*, 13.

130. Guiley, *The Encyclopedia of Ghosts and Spirits*, 320–321.

131. Ibid, 353.

132. Guiley, *Harper's Encyclopedia of Mystical and Paranormal Experience*, 555–556.

133. Guiley, *The Encyclopedia of Ghosts and Spirits*, 6.

134. Ibid.

135. Kenney, "Stalking the Afterlife."

136. Guiley, *The Encyclopedia of Ghosts and Spirits*, 332–333.

137. Guiley, *The Encyclopedia of Ghosts and* Spirits, 324.

138. Guiley, *The Encyclopedia of* Ghosts *and Spirits*.

139. "Loyd Auerbach: Paranormal Investigator and Author," The Paranormal Network. http://www.mindreader.com/loyd (accessed May 24, 2006, 1).

140. Ibid.

141. Ibid.

142. Ibid.

143. "The Veritas Research Program," University of Arizona. http://veritas.arizona.edu.

144. Joseph Darwin, "Confusing an Item of Faith with Science," Joseph

Darwin Official Web Site. http://joe.darwin.net/Schwartz.html.

145. Edward, *Crossing Over: The Stories Behind the Stories*, 110–111.

146. Ibid, 125.

147. Guiley, *The Encyclopedia of Ghosts and Spirits*, 189.

148. Guiley, *The Encyclopedia of Ghosts and Spirits*, 190.

149. Brian Carnell, "John Edward's Cold Reading Gig," Skepticism.net. http://www.skepti cism.net/articles/2001/000012.html (accessed January 26, 2006).

150. Michael Shermer, "Deconstructing the Dead: Crossing Over One Last Time to Expose Medium John Edward," *E-Skeptic*, February 27, 2001. http://the-light.com/archive /mens/threads/79855.html (accessed January 23, 2006).

151. Michael Shermer, "Does James Van Praagh Talk to the Dead? Nope! Fraud! Part 2," from "Talking Twaddle with the Dead," *Skeptic* magazine. Also available online at http://www.holysmoke.org/praagh2.htm (accessed January 23, 2006).

152. Shermer, "Does James Van Praagh Talk to the Dead? Nope! Fraud! Part 2."

153. "James Randi," Answers.com. http://www.answers.com/topic/james-randi.

154. Ibid.

155. Ibid.

156. James Randi, "Sylvia Browne Is a Liar," *Swift*, the online newsletter of the James Randi Educational Foundation, March

5, 2004. http://www.randi.org/jr/030504newsweek .html (accessed January 25, 2006).

157. Sylvia Browne, The Official Site. http://www.sylvia.org/home/index.cfm (accessed January 25, 2006).

158. "About CSICOP," Committee for the Scientific Investigation of Claims of the Paranormal. http://www.csicop.org/about (accessed October 21, 2006).

159. Guiley, *The Encyclopedia of Ghosts and Spirits*, 77–78.

160. "Demystifying John Edward of *Crossing Over*," John Edward: Truth or Scam? http://www.re-quest.net/entertainment/movies-and-tv/tv/john-edward (accessed January 25, 2006).

161. Edward, *Crossing Over: The Stories Behind the Stories*, 115.

162. Michael Shermer, "CSICOP Routs Psychics on *Larry King Live*," Skeptical News for 8 March 2001: Archive of Previous NTS Skeptical News Listings. http://www.ntskept ics.org/news/news2001-03-08.htm (accessed January 23, 2006).

163. Gruber, "An Enlightenment Interview with Dean Radin, Ph.D.," 1.

164. Guiley, *Harper's Encyclopedia of Mystical and Paranormal Experience*, 612–613.

165. Ibid, 65.

166. Edward Hower, "A Spirited Story of the Psychic and the Colonel," *Smithsonian* magazine, May 1, 1995, 122–123.

167. Ibid, 124.

168. Vernon Harrison, "H.P. Blavatsky and the SPR: An Examination of

the Hodgson Report of 1885" (Pasadena, Calif.: Theosophical University Press, 1997). Also available online at http://www.theosociety.org/pasadena/hpb-spr/hpbspr-h.htm, pp.

169. Matt Roper, "Spooky Truth: TV's *Most Haunted* Con Exposed," Mirror.co.uk, October 28, 2005. http://www.mirror.co.uk/news/topstories/tm_objectid=16303507&method=full&siteid94762-name_page.html.

170. DuBois, *Don't Kiss Them Good-bye*, 50.

171. Ibid, 50–54.

172. Ibid, 58–63.

173. Ibid, 65–66.

174. Chris Dufresne, *My Psychic Journey* (Carlsbad, Calif.: Hay House Inc., 2006), 74–79.

175. Van Praagh, *Talking to Heaven: A Medium's Message of Life After Death*, 22–23.

176. Nathaniel Friedland, *Be Psychic Now! Fast, Easy, Sensible ESP Method—Even Works for Skeptics* (San Francisco: LionStar Press, 1999), 77.

177. William W. Hewitt, *Psychic Development for Beginners: An Easy Guide to Releasing and Developing Your Psychic Abilities* (Woodbury, Minn.: Llewellyn Publications, 2005), 1.

178. Ibid, 49–56.

179. Huson, *How to Test and Develop Your ESP*, 43.

180. Guiley, *Harper's Encyclopedia of Mystical and Paranormal Experience*, 546.

181. Huson, *How to Test and Develop Your ESP*, 43–46.

182. Ibid, 45–48.

183. Ibid, 57–58.

184. Eason, *The Complete Guide to Psychic Development*, 43–44.

185. Guiley, *Harper's Encyclopedia of Mystical and Paranormal Experience*, 470.

186. Eason, *The Complete Guide to Psychic Development*, 45.

187. Huson, *How to Test and Develop Your ESP*, 18.

188. Rupert Sheldrake, *Dogs That Know When Their Owners Are Coming Home* (New York: Three Rivers Press, 1999), 54–63.

189. Ibid, 19.

190. Ibid, 80–81.

191. Ibid, 7.

192. Adele von Rusf McCormick, Marlena Deborah McCormick, and Thomas E. McCormick, *Horses and the Mystical Path: The Celtic Way of Expanding the Human Soul* (Novato, Calif.: New World Library, 2004), 3–4.

193. Sheldrake, *Dogs That Know When Their Owners Are Coming Home*, 233–234.

194. Owen Courreges, "Dogs Can Detect Cancer, Study Shows," ChronicallyBiased.com. http://www.chronicallybiased.com/indexphp?itemid=1658.

195. Elizabeth Cohen, "Woman Says Dog Detected Her Cancer," CNN.com. http://www.c n.com/2006/HEALTH/conditons/02/06/cohen.dogcancerdetect/ndex.html.

196. Ibid.

197. Sheldrake, *Dogs That Know When Their Owners Are Coming Home*, 245.

198. Ibid, 247.

199. Heaven Ross and Howard G. Charing, "Psychic Results from … House Plants?," adapted from *Plant Spirit Shamanism*, 2006. Also available online at http://www.care2.c om/channels/solutions/outdoors/3051.

200. Ibid, 2.

201. William Lee Rand, "Reiki Research," The International Center for Reiki Training. http://www.reiki.org/reikinews/reikin24.html.

202. "Sonya Fitzpatrick," biography, available online at http://www.eetv.com/sonya-fitzpatrick/person/173008/biography.html, downloaded November 14, 2006, pp. 1–2.

203. Cesar Millan with Melissa Jo Peltier, *Cesar's Way* (New York: Harmony Books, 2006), 198–214.

204. Mark Derr, "Pack of Lies," *The New York Times*, August 31, 2006.

205. Sheldrake, *Dogs That Know When Their Owners Are Coming Home*, 19.

Further Resources

BOOKS

Browne, Sylvia. *Psychic Children: Revealing the Intuitive Gifts and Hidden Abilities of Boys and Girls.* New York: Dutton, 2007.

Remembering her own psychic experiences as a child, Browne looks at kids with special abilities and asks adults to encourage and support them.

Browne, Sylvia, and Chris Dufresne. *Spirit of Animals.* Cincinnati: Angel Bea Publishing, 2007.

Browne and her son and business partner Dufresne discuss whether animals are psychic, do they communicate after death, and do they possess souls.

DuBois, Allison. *Don't Kiss Them Good-bye.* New York: A Fireside Book, 2004.

In DuBois' very personal first book, she talks about how alone and different she always felt as an adolescent, and how parents can identify psychic children and help them develop their gifts.

Dufresne, Chris. *My Psychic Journey.* Carlsbad, Calif: Hay House Inc., 2006.

Sometimes it's difficult for a child to step out of the parent's shadow, but Dufresne, son of Sylvia Browne, has become a successful psychic and father to a highly gifted daughter.

Guiley, Rosemary Ellen. *Encyclopedia of the Strange, Mystical and Unexplained.* New York: Gramercy Books, 2001.

Guiley has written several one-volume encyclopedias about the paranormal, but this book may contain nearly anything the reader desires to know about unexplained phenomena.

Rain, Mary Summer. *In Your Dreams: The Ultimate Dream Dictionary.* Charlottesville, Va.: Hampton Roads Publishing, 2005.

An update to Rain's *Guide to Dream Symbols,* this edition offers over 20,000 symbols, from A to Z, to help with dream interpretation.

Ross, Scarlett. *Nostradamus for Dummies.* Hoboken, N.J.: For Dummies Publishing, 2005.

For someone who's been gone for more than 400 years, Nostradamus remains in the news as perhaps the best prognosticator of all time. This book covers all the bases—as well as the hoaxes—of Nostradamus' long-running popularity.

Shaw, Maria. *Maria Shaw's Tarot for Teens.* Woodbury, Minn.: Llewellyn Publications, 2004.

Shaw looks at the history of the strangely beautiful Tarot cards, their development into the Major and Minor Arcana, how to lay out card spreads for divination, and even how to conduct a reading session and interpret what the cards say.

AUDIO

Browne, Sylvia. *Life on the Other Side: A Psychic's Tour of the Afterlife.* 2005.

A fascinating voyage to all the beautiful cities, scenery, and people that Sylvia Browne visualizes in Heaven. Available as CD, audiocassette or MP3 download.

Edward, John. *Developing Your Own Psychic Powers.* 2003.

A six-CD set, this complete guide to becoming psychic covers meditation, psychic self-defense, angels and spirit guides, and even explains how to hold a sitting. Other formats include audiocassette and download for MP3 players.

Van Praagh, James. *Talking to Heaven: A Medium's Message of Life After Death.* 1998.

This is the story that inspired John Edward to write a book. Van Praagh's first psychic experience is not only amazing but confirms his message of love, acceptance, and the presence of the "god spark" in all of us. Available in audiocassette.

Bibliography

"About CSICOP." Committee for the Scientific Investigation of Claims of the Paranormal. Available online at http://www.csicop.org/about. Downloaded October 21, 2006.

"About Lisa." Lifetime. Available online at http://www.lifetimetv.com/shows/lisawilliams/bio/index.php. Downloaded November 7, 2006.

"About the Society." The American Society for Psychical Research. Available online at http://www.aspr.com/who.htm.

Achtemeier, Paul J., gen. ed. *Harper's Bible Dictionary.* San Francisco: Harper & Row, 1985.

Acorah, Derek. *The Psychic Adventures of Derek Acorah.* London: HarperElement, 2004.

"Allison DuBois Editorial Commentary." Available online at http://www.allison dubois.com/news.html.

"Allison DuBois: *Medium* TV Show Based on Her Life." Available online at http://phoenix.about.com/od/famous/a/dubois.htm. Downloaded May 24, 2006.

Barry, Dan. "For Once, a Psychic Looks Back." *The New York Times.* April 12, 2006.

Browne, Sylvia. *Life on the Other Side: A Psychic's Tour of the Afterlife.* New York: Dutton Publishing, 2000.

Carnell, Brian. "John Edward's Cold Reading Gig," Skepticism.Net. Available online at http://www.skepticism.net/articles/2001/000012.html. Downloaded January 26, 2006.

Cheatham, Eric. "Quatrains of Nostradamus: Interpretation." Available online at http://www.crystalinks.com/quatraininterpretations.html.

Clarke, Susanna. *Jonathan Strange and Mr. Norrell.* New York: Bloomsbury Publishing, 2004.

Cohen, Elizabeth. "Woman Says Dog Detected Her Cancer." CNN.com: HEALTH. February 6, 2006. Available online at http://www.cnn.com/2006/HEALTH/conditons/02/06/cohen.dogcancerdetect/ndex.html.

Courreges, Owen. "Dogs Can Detect Cancer, Study Shows." Chronically Biased.com. Available online at http://www.chronicallybiased.com/indexphp?itemid=1658.

Davis, Kenneth C. *Don't Know Much About Mythology.* New York: HarperCollins, 2005.

"Demystifying John Edward of *Crossing Over.*" John Edward: Truth or Scam? Available online at http://www.re-quest.net/entertainment/movies-and-tv/tv/john-edward. Downloaded January 25, 2006.

Derr, Mark. "Pack of Lies." *The New York Times,* August 31, 2006.

Dirks, Tom. "*The Exorcist* (1973)." Available online at http://www.filmsite.org/exor2.html.

DuBois, Allison. *Don't Kiss Them Good-bye.* New York: A Fireside Book, 2004.

Dufresne, Chris. *My Psychic Journey.* Carlsbad, Calif.: Hay House Inc., 2006.

Eason, Cassandra. *The Complete Guide to Psychic Development.* Berkeley, Calif.: Crossing Press, 2003.

Edward, John. *Crossing Over: The Stories Behind the Stories.* San Diego: Jodere Group Inc., 2001.

"Emanuel Swedenborg (1688-1772)," Books and Writers. Available online at http://www.kirjasto.sci.fi/sweden.htm.

Farha, Bryan. "Sylvia Browne: Psychic Guru or Quack?" Quackwatch Home Page. Available online at http://www.quackwatch.org/11Ind/browne.html. Downloaded January 25, 2006.

Fiddler on the Roof (1971). Internet Movie database. Available online at http://www.imdb.com/title/tt0067093/combined#content.

Foster, Robert. *Tolkien's World from A to Z: The Complete Guide to Middle-Earth.* New York: Del Ray Books, 1978.

Franklin, Nancy. "Boy Detective." *The New Yorker,* July 10 and 17, 2006.

Friedland, Nathaniel. *Be Psychic Now! Fast, Easy, Sensible ESP Method—Even Works for Skeptics.* San Francisco: LionStar Press, 1999.

"*Ghostbusters* (1984)." Internet Movie Database. Available online at http://www. imdb.com/title/tt0087332.

Gruber, Jordan S. "An Enlightenment Interview with Dean Radin, Ph.D." Available online at http://www.enlightenment.com/media/interviews/radin.html. Downloaded December 5, 2006.

Guiley, Rosemary Ellen. *The Angels Tarot.* San Francisco: Harper San Francisco, 1995.

———. *The Encyclopedia of Ghosts and Spirits*, second edition. New York: Facts on File, 2000.

———. *Encyclopedia of the Strange, Mystical and Unexplained.* New York: Gramercy Books, 2001.

———. *Harper's Encyclopedia of Mystical and Paranormal Experience.* San Francisco: Harper San Francisco, 1991.

———. "Luck, Psi and Lotteries—Part II." Visionary Living, first appeared in *FATE* Magazine, September 2004. Available online at http://www.visionary living.com/articles/luckpsi-II.php.

Hamilton, Edith. *Mythology.* Boston: Little, Brown & Co., 1942.

Harris, Tom. "How Nostradamus Works: It's Good to Know." Available online at http//science.howstuffworks.com/nostradamus.htm.

Harrison, Vernon. "H.P. Blavatsky and the SPR: An Examination of the Hodgson Report of 1885." Pasadena, Calif.: Theosophical University Press, 1997. Available online at http://www.theosociety.org/pasadena/hpb-spr/hpbspr-h.htm.

Hewitt, William W. *Psychic Development for Beginners: An Easy Guide to Releasing and Developing Your Psychic Abilities.* Woodbury, Minn.: Llewellyn Publications, 2005.

Hower, Edward. "A Spirited Story of the Psychic and the Colonel." *Smithsonian* magazine, May 1, 1995.

Huson, Paul. *How to Test and Develop Your ESP.* Lanham, Md.: Madison Books, 2001.

Hyman, Ray. "How *Not* to Test Mediums." Skeptical Inquirer, January/February 2003. Committee for Skeptical Inquiry. Available online at http://www.csicop. org/si/2003-01/medium.html.

"James Randi." Occultism and Parapsyschology on Answers.com. Available online at http://www.answers.com/topic/james-randi.

"James Van Praagh Biography." The official Web site. Available online at http://www.vanpraagh.com. Downloaded January 23, 2006.

"Jeane Dixon." Internet Movie Database. Available online at http://www.imdb.com/name/nm02280864. Downloaded August 24, 2006.

"*John Edward/Cross Country* on WE; Season Begins August 25, 2006," The official Web site worldwide. Available online at http://www.johnedward.net/about_John_Edward.htm.

Kenney, Michael. "Stalking the Afterlife." *Zest* magazine, *The Houston Chronicle*, September 10, 2006.

"The Laci Peterson Case." CourtTV Online. Available online at http://www.courttv.com/talk/chat_transcripts/2004/0722peterson-renier.html. Downloaded January 30, 2006.

"Loyd Auerbach: Paranormal Investigator and Author." The Paranormal Network. Available online at http://www.mindreader.com/loyd. Downloaded May 24, 2006.

Mackay, Charles. *Extraordinary Popular Delusions and the Madness of Crowds.* New York: Farrar, Straus and Giroux, 1932.

McCormick, Adele von Rusf, Marlena Deborah McCormick, and Thomas E. McCormick. *Horses and the Mystical Path: The Celtic Way of Expanding the Human Soul.* Novato, Calif.: New World Library, 2004.

McFadden, Dr. Dennis. "Psychic Detectives." The Skeptic's Dictionary. Available online at https://webspace.utexas.edu/cokerwr/www/index.html/detectives.shtml. Downloaded October 21, 2006.

McMoneagle, Joseph. *Memoirs of a Psychic Spy: The Remarkable Life of U.S. Government Remote Viewer 001.* Charlottesville, Va.: Hampton Roads Publishing, 2006.

"Media and Publications." Available online at http://www.after-death.com.

"Medium: We See Dead People." Biography Channel, July 8, 2006.

"Memorable Quotes from *The Bullwinkle Show* (1961)." The Internet Movie Database. Available online at http://www.imdb.com/titles/tt0054524/quotes.

Millan, Cesar, with Melissa Jo Peltier. *Cesar's Way.* New York: Harmony Books, 2006.

"9/11/01: Tragedy in the US." Morgana's Observatory. Available online at http://www.dreamscape.com/morgana/91101.htm.

Nisbet, Matt. "Talking to Heaven Through Television: How the Mass Media Package and Sell Psychic Medium John Edward." Generation sXeptic, Committee for the Scientific Investigation of Claims of the Paranormal, March 13, 2001. Available online at http://www.csicop.org/genx/edward. Downloaded January 25, 2006.

"Nostradamus' Biography." Available online at http://www.crystalinks.com/nostradamus.html. Downloaded August 21, 2006.

"Psychic detective," The Skeptic's Dictionary. Available online at http://skepdic.com/psychdet.html.

"Psychic Jeane Dixon Dies." SHOWBIZ on CNN Interactive. Available online at http://www.CNN.com/SHOWBIZ/9701/26/dixon. Downloaded August 24, 2006.

Rand, William Lee. "Reiki Research." Available online at http://www.reiki.org/reikinews/reikin24.html.

Randi, James. "Sylvia Browne Is a Liar." *Swift*, the online newsletter of the James Randi Educational Foundation, March 5, 2004. Available online at http://www.randi.org/jr/030504newsweek.html. Downloaded January 25, 2006.

———. "Derek Revealed—Again." *Swift*, the online newsletter of the James Randi Educational Foundation, November 11, 2005. Available online at www.randi.org/jr/200511/111105derek.html. Downloaded January 25, 2006.

Renier, Noreen, with Naomi Lucks. *A Mind for Murder: The Real-Life Files of a Psychic Investigator.* New York: Berkley Books, 2005.

Roll, William G., and Valerie Storey. *Unleashed: Of Poltergeists and Murder, the Curious Story of Tina Resch.* New York: Paraview Pocket Books, 2004.

Roper, Matt. "Spooky Truth: TV's *Most Haunted* Con Exposed TV." Mirror.co.uk, October 28, 2005. Available online at http://www.mirror.co.uk/news/topstories/tm_objectid=16303507&method=full8siteid=94762-name_page.html. Downloaded November 16, 2005.

Ross, Heaven, and Howard G. Charing. "Psychic Results from . . . House Plants?" Adapted from *Plant Spirit Shamanism*, 2006. Available online at http://www.care2.com/channels/solutions/outdoors/3051.

Schwartz, Stephan A., and The Mobius Group. "A Preliminary Survey of the Eastern Harbor, Alexandria, Egypt Including a Comparison of Side Scan Sonar and Remote Viewing." Abstract of report delivered to Annual Meeting of the Society for Underwater Archaeology, January 11, 1980. Available online at http://www.stephanaschwartz.com/home.htm.

Shermer, Michael. "CSICOP Routs Psychics on *Larry King Live*." Skeptical News for 8 March 2001: Archive of Previous NTS Skeptical News Listings. Available online at http://www.ntskeptics.org/news/news2001-03-08.htm. Downloaded January 23, 2006.

———."Deconstructing the Dead: Crossing Over One Last Time to Expose Medium John Edward." Off Topic: John Edward, posted by Hair Religion, August 24, 2004, originally published in *E-Skeptic*, February 27, 2001. Available online at http://the-light.com/archive/mens/threads/79855.html. Downloaded January 23, 2006.

———. "Does James Van Praagh Talk to the Dead? Nope! Fraud!" Part 2, from "Talking Twaddle with the Dead," *Skeptic* magazine. Available online at http://www.holysmoke.org/praagh2.htm. Downloaded January 23, 2006.

"Sonya Fitzpatrick." Biography. Available online at http://www.tv.com/sonya-fitzpatrick/person/173008/biography.html. Downloaded November 14, 2006.

Swedenborg, Emanuel. *De Verbo*. Translated by Whitehead, note 3. Available online at http://www.heavenlydoctrines.org/Scripts/dtSearch. Downloaded October 21, 2006.

———. *Heaven and Hell*. Translated by Ager, notes 340 and 384. Available online at http://www.heavenlydoctrines.org/Scripts/dtSearch. Downloaded October 21, 2006.

———. *True Christian Religion*. Translated by Ager, notes 805 and 809. Available online at http://www.heavenlydoctrines.org/Scripts/dtSearch. Downloaded October 21, 2006.

———. *True Christian Religion*. Translated by Chadwick, note 794. Available online at http://www.heavenlydoctrines.org/Scripts/dtSearch. Downloaded October 21, 2006.

Trachtenberg, Jeffrey A. "In Publishing, One Medium Looms Large." *The Wall Street Journal*, March 29, 2006.

Van Praagh, James. *Talking to Heaven: A Medium's Message of Life After Death*. New York: Dutton Publishers, 1997.

"The Veritas Research Program." University of Arizona. Available online at http://veritas.arizona.edu.

Index

About the Author

JOANNE P. AUSTIN has been writing about the paranormal for 20 years, working with her friend Rosemary Ellen Guiley on several books that explore the mysteries of ghosts and mediums, alchemists and exorcisms, vampires and witches, saints and angels. Each collaboration has been a magical experience. Austin lives in Texas with her husband and two daughters, all three of whom are deeply intuitive, very creative, and occasionally psychic.

About the Consulting Editor

ROSEMARY ELLEN GUILEY is one of the foremost authorities on the paranormal. Psychic experiences in childhood led to her lifelong study and research of paranormal mysteries. A journalist by training, she has worked full time in the paranormal since 1983, as an author, presenter, and investigator. She has written 31 nonfiction books on paranormal topics, translated into 13 languages, and hundreds of articles. She has experienced many of the phenomena she has researched. She has appeared on numerous television, documentary, and radio shows. She is also a member of the League of Paranormal Gentlemen for Spooked Productions, a columnist for *TAPS Paramagazine*, a consulting editor for *FATE* magazine, and writer for the "Paranormal Insider" blog. Ms. Guiley's books include *The Encyclopedia of Angels, The Encyclopedia of Magic and Alchemy, The Encyclopedia of Saints, The Encyclopedia of Vampires, Werewolves, and Other Monsters,* and *The Encyclopedia of Witches and Witchcraft*, all from Facts On File. She lives in Maryland and her Web site is http://www.visionaryliving.com.